In the

Vanguard of Reform

IN THE
VANGUARD OF REFORM

Russia's Enlightened Bureaucrats 1825–1861

W. Bruce Lincoln

DeKalb
Northern Illinois University Press

Publication of this book was assisted by a grant from the Publications Program of the National Endowment for the Humanities, an independent federal agency.

Library of Congress Cataloging in Publication Data

Lincoln, W. Bruce
    In the vanguard of reform.

    Bibliography: p.
    1. Soviet Union—Politics and government—1825–1855.   2. Soviet Union—Politics and government—1855–1881.   3. Bureaucracy—Soviet Union—History—19th century.   4. Soviet Union—Economic policy.   5. Soviet Union—Social policy.   I. Title.
JN6511.L55   947'.073   82–6509
ISBN 0-87580-084-X   AACR2
ISBN 0-87580-536-1 (pbk.)

To Bruce McCully and Bill Abbot, my first history teachers, and to Lee and Carol Congdon, two uncommon friends

Contents

List of Abbreviations

ANSSSR	Arkhiv Akademii Nauk S.S.S.R. (Leningrad)
CU/AREEHC	Columbia University. Archive of Russian and East European History and Culture (New York City)
GIALO	Gosudarstvennyi Istoricheskii Arkhiv Leningradskoi Oblasti. (Leningrad)
GIM	Gosudarstvennyi Istoricheskii Muzei. Otdel rukopisei (Moscow)
GPB	Gosudarstvennaia Publichnaia Biblioteka imeni M. E. Saltykova-Shchedrina. Otdel rukopisei (Leningrad)
IV	*Istoricheskii vestnik.* St. Petersburg, 1880–1914
LN	*Literaturnoe nasledstvo.* Moscow, 1931—
ORGBL	Gosudarstvennaia Biblioteka S.S.S.R. imeni V. I. Lenina. Otdel rukopisei (Moscow)
OZ	*Otechestvennye zapiski.* St. Petersburg, 1829–1884
PD	Institut Russkoi Literatury (Pushkinskii Dom) Akademii Nauk S.S.S.R. (Leningrad)
PRO	Public Records Office (London)
PSZ **sobranie 1-oe**	*Polnoe sobranie zakonov Rossiiskoi Imperii s 1849g.* Sobranie pervoe. 45 vols. St. Petersburg, 1830
PSZ **sobranie 2-oe**	*Polnoe sobranie zakonov Rossiiskoi Imperii.* Sobranie vtoroe. 55 vols. St. Petersburg, 1830–1882
RA	*Russkii arkhiv.* Moscow, 1863–1917
RBS	*Russkii biograficheskii slovar'.* 25 vols. St. Petersburg, 1896–1918.

Abbreviations

RS	*Russkaia starina.* St. Petersburg, 1870–1918
RV	*Russkii vestnik.* Moscow–St. Petersburg, 1856–1906
SIRIO	*Sbornik Imperatorskago Russkago Istoricheskago Obshchestva.* St. Petersburg–Iur'ev–Moscow, 1867–1916
TsGALI	Tsentral'nyi Gosudarstvennyi Arkhiv Literatury i Iskusstva S.S.S.R. (Moscow)
TsGAOR	Tsentral'nyi Gosudarstvennyi Arkhiv Oktiabr'skoi Revoliutsii (Moscow)
TsGIAL	Tsentral'nyi Gosudarstvennyi Istoricheskii Arkhiv S.S.S.R. (Leningrad)
VE	*Vestnik evropy.* St. Petersburg, 1866–1918
Velikaia reforma	A. K. Dzhivelegov, A. S. Melgunov, and V. I. Picheta, eds. *Velikaia reforma. Russkoe obshchestvo i krest'ianskii vopros v proshlom i nastoiashchem.* 6 vols. Moscow, 1911
ZhMGI	*Zhurnal Ministerstva Gosudarstvennykh Imushchestv.* St. Petersburg, 1841–1918
ZhMIu	*Zhurnal Ministerstva Iustitsii.* St. Petersburg, 1859–1868, 1894–1915
ZhMVD	*Zhurnal Ministerstva Vnutrennikh Del.* St. Petersburg, 1829–1861

Preface

The first decade of Alexander II's reign is known in Russian history as the Era of the Great Reforms, a time quite properly thought of by historians as the major era of social, economic, and institutional transformation in Russia between the reign of Peter the Great and the Revolution of 1905. Coming directly after the notoriously repressive last decade of the Nicholas era, the appearance of such a dramatic period of reform and transformation has led scholars to seek its causes in dramatic events. Surely some great, even cataclysmic, force must have driven Alexander II and his advisers to initiate what appeared to be such an astonishing change in policy. Historians, therefore, generally have focused upon two phenomena, one dramatic and, for Russian opinion, shocking; the other, less dramatic, but perhaps potentially more worrisome for mid-nineteenth-century Russian statesmen. The first of these was Russia's defeat in the Crimean War by a relatively small, ineptly commanded Allied expeditionary force. The second was the increasingly frequent serf revolts that the Empire experienced throughout the 1850s.

For such turn-of-the-century historians as Aleksandr Kornilov, the reason for the apparently dramatic change in the attitudes of Alexander II and his advisers after 1856 was to be found in the crisis of confidence brought on by the Crimean defeat itself. Russians were so shocked by the defeat, Kornilov insisted, that they demanded broad reforms, while Alexander II was so shaken that he was willing to heed their demands rather than punish the men who expressed them by arrest or exile as his iron-willed father would have done.[1] Soviet historians and, most recently, Iu. I. Gerasimova and others associated with M. V. Nechkina's symposium on the revolutionary situation in Russia during the early years of Alexander II's reign have argued that an even broader crisis, brought on by widespread serf revolts and the failings of the serf-based Russian economy, forced the Emperor and his counselors to initiate a broad reformist policy.[2] Only P. A. Zaionchkovskii, perhaps the greatest living Soviet specialist on nineteenth-century Russia, refrains from isolating one particular reason for the onset of the Great Reform era and sees it as the result of a variety of more complex factors.[3]

Western historians have tended to accept one or the other of these explanations, or they have combined the two in some way. As Terence Emmons wrote in the mid-1960s, "There are two overriding considerations to be perceived in the state's motivations for undertaking emancipation: concern for economic development, and a desire to ensure social and political stability. Both were directly related to the experience of Russia's defeat in the Crimean War."[4] On a somewhat differerent, though less well documented note, Alfred Rieber argued, also in the mid-1960s, that the Crimean defeat, coupled with its attendant fiscal crisis, convinced Alexander II that Russia required a modern military establishment patterned on the Prussian model and, because such an army had a large ready-reserve component, it could not be established until the Russian serfs were emancipated.[5] Finally, Daniel Field has explained that serfdom fell "by stages" as a consequence of the Imperial legislative process and that that process went forward because "nineteenth-century Russian serfdom lacked supporting ideological and political structures."[6] Field's work describes more accurately than earlier efforts by western scholars the process by which serfdom fell; yet it still does not explain fully why or how the reform process went forward so rapidly and effectively in the late 1850s and early 1860s.

All of these arguments, except for that set forth by Field, share the common assumption that the economic failings of serfdom, the problem of preserving political stability, and the need to restore Russia's tarnished military prestige were the major forces that impelled Alexander II's government to embark on a reformist path. Yet, while Alexander and his advisers obviously concluded that Russia's military establishment must be modernized and considered it essential to preserve the domestic peace that had been threatened by the widespread serf revolts of the 1850s, the broader issue of whether these factors actually impelled them to initiate the process of social, administrative, and economic transformation is much more complex. None of the ministers, nor even Alexander II himself, thought serf revolts dangerously threatening in 1856, and the Russian nobility were generally willing to take their chances with the ever-present threat of peasant violence, just as were plantation owners in the American antebellum South.[7] Likewise, the Crimean defeat posed no great threat to Russia's territorial integrity, and it raised no unusual concern about national security in the minds of Russia's policy-makers. Stated most simply, although the Crimean defeat and increased serf revolts may have made Alexander II and his advisers more aware of the need for reform, there is not much evidence to indicate that these factors made them feel any acute sense of urgency about embarking on a dramatic program of social and economic transformation.

Questions such as these cast doubt on the argument that a crisis of policy and a failure of Russia's servile economy impelled Alexander and his advisers along a previously uncharted reformist path. Equally important, the Great Reform legislation simply was too complex and required too much sophisticated knowledge about the Empire's economic, administrative, and judicial affairs to have been formulated in the short period of time between Alexander II's famous speech to the Moscow nobility in March 1856, and late 1862, when the bulk of the draft legislation was completed. To put the matter another way, one well might ask how the Russian bureaucracy, which contemporaries and historians have condemned as ponderous, inefficient, and corrupt, could have produced such a vast corpus of reform legislation in the space of about five years. After all, Catherine II and her advisers had devoted a full quarter-century to the much less complex task of restructuring Russia's administrative institutions and, in that time, had completed only the portion of the reform that dealt with provincial administration. Likewise, it had taken Alexander I and his counselors more than a decade to restructure Russia's central administration to coincide with that provincial apparatus Catherine had created. In the second quarter of the nineteenth century, Nicholas I and his "Chief of Staff for Peasant Affairs," Count Kiselev, had devoted nearly two decades to reforming the institutions and procedures with which they administered Russia's state peasants, and even so astute an administrator as the great Speranskii had needed nearly a decade to compile and codify Russia's laws. All of these were far less complex tasks, with significantly less far-reaching implications, than the Great Reform legislation of the 1860s.

Given this consistent record of glacially slow performance in dealing with comparatively less complex tasks of administrative reorganization and reform, how did the Russian bureaucracy draft, in the space of a mere half-decade, that vast body of Great Reform legislation that altered fundamentally the Empire's social, economic, and judicial order? The answer to this question cannot be found in Russia's Crimean defeat, nor can it be found in the crisis of her servile economy. It cannot be found in the personality of Alexander II, nor in the growing reformist sentiment expressed by educated Russians: Alexander II had neither the strength of character nor the powerful personality of his father; and the reformist sentiment that surged so dramatically to the fore among educated Russians on the eve of the Emancipation of 1861, emerged *after* Alexander's famous Moscow speech about the need to resolve the serf issue, not before it. Indeed, thinking Russians had greeted Alexander's accession with only modest expectations for change and the most minimal hopes for reform.[8] In 1855, no one in Russia, and Alexander II least of all, even remotely imagined that the Great Reforms would become an accomplished fact just more than a half-decade after the Crimean War ended.[9]

To answer more satisfactorily the questions about how the body of the Great Reform legislation was produced, and why it assumed the shape it did, we must look back to the era of Nicholas I and, especially, to its last decade, which historians generally have considered to be one of the most reactionary periods in Imperial Russia's history. Beginning in the late 1830s, an unusual group of young officials, whom I have identified in this study as enlightened bureaucrats, began to appear in St. Petersburg's chanceries. Such men held different attitudes about state service and reform than did most government officials. They rejected as useless those formalistic routines and rituals that had become so much a part of Russia's bureaucratic world by the 1840s[10] and demanded efficiency and innovation rather than time-honored custom in administration. Most of all, because they believed in a more aggressive sort of administration than did most bureaucrats, they quickly perceived that the information needed to formulate workable policies simply did not exist in Russia's central administrative offices. Therefore, one of their major activities during the 1840s became the collection of information about social, economic, and administrative conditions in Russia's provinces that was unlike any assembled by Russian officials before.

Increased quantities of more accurate data about Russian social and economic conditions were not in themselves sufficient to set the stage for the Great Reform legislation, although they were one of its prerequisites. Perhaps even more important, the enlightened bureaucrats' view of change had to evolve beyond that held by their mentors and superiors to one that perceived the need for a far broader and more fundamental transformation than even the most progressive Russian statesmen envisioned during the Nicholas era. Such a view, however, had to be firmly grounded in experience and not based mainly on theory, as was the case with the reform views held by most of the intelligentsia at the time. What that view was, how and why the enlightened bureaucrats developed it, how it came to exercise a decisive influence on the content of the Great Reform legislation, and how it was related to the unique institutional structure that emerged in the mid-nineteenth-century Russian state are some of the major questions that this volume will examine.

W. Bruce Lincoln
Sycamore, Illinois
New Year's Day, 1982

Acknowledgments

It would require a great deal more space than is available here to acknowledge the generosity and kindness of the many people who have in some way aided my efforts to write this book. Marc Raeff, Leopold Haimson, and Daniel Orlovsky have read and commented on several versions of this manuscript over the years, and their encouragement, combined with gentle urgings, have in large part been responsible for my seeing the task through to its end. Daniel Field, David Macey, and Richard Robbins read earlier versions of the manuscript, while Jacob Kipp and JoAnn Ruckman read parts of it at different times. All offered generous comments that helped to improve it, and whatever virtues it may have are in large part due to their collective wisdom.

In addition to these American scholars, Petr Andreevich Zaionchkovskii deserves special mention. Not only has he offered me the benefit of generous scholarly counsel over many years, but he has served above and beyond the call of duty as my guide in learning about the many complex archival sources that related to the problems discussed in this book. Without his help, it would have been more than difficult to assemble the materials needed to begin to tell the story of Russia's enlightened bureaucrats.

During the past decade or so, I also have benefited greatly from discussions about the problems explored in this volume with many other scholars in the United States, the Soviet Union, and Poland. In this, Ludwik Bazylow, Helju Bennett, Valentina Chernukha, Lee Congdon, Ralph Fisher, Brenda Meehan-Waters, Sidney Monas, Franciszka Ramotowska, Charles Timberlake, and Richard Wortman are at the top of what is, to my good fortune, a lengthy list. These and others too numerous to list have helped me to focus my explorations of the problems related to the enlightened bureaucrats in Russia.

Here at Northern Illinois University I have had many sorts of support over the years, for which I am indeed grateful. Carroll Moody, our department chairman during most of the years when I was working on this volume, has been generous in his efforts to juggle teaching schedules in order to give me the time I needed to write, and, on more than one occasion, he has shielded me from onerous committee duties when I needed to be free of such administrative entanglements. Since his arrival here several years ago, George Gutsche, my colleague in nineteenth-century Russian literature, has been a source of wise counsel and good humor, both of which I have appreciated far more than may have been evident on some occasions. In recent years, I also have profited from the logistical and financial support that I have received from an unusual group of senior administrators, all of them accomplished scholars in their own right, who have assembled here to direct the course of a university that has been in the throes of transition. Among them, I particularly want to thank William Monat, James Norris, Jon Miller, John LaTourette, and Dean Jaros, all of whom have supported my work in important ways on more than one occasion. Finally, but certainly not least, I owe much more than ritualistic thanks to Mary Livingston, director of Northern Illinois University Press. I am grateful indeed for her helpful efficiency in getting this volume into print.

My wife Patti deserves her own special paragraph of thanks in any acknowledgment of the help I have received in writing this book. Her good humor and good sense, not to mention her willingness to put up with my quirks and foibles, have helped more than I can express here.

Institutions, too, have been generous in supporting the research that went into this book, and my debt to them is very great. Grants from the International Research and Exchanges Board and the Fulbright-Hays Faculty Research Abroad Program supported my research in the archives of Leningrad and Moscow on several visits to the Soviet Union during which the Academy of Sciences of the U.S.S.R. and the Institutes of History at Moscow and Leningrad State Universities served as generous and helpful hosts. Likewise, the Historical Institute at the University of Warsaw outdid itself in making me welcome during a term as a Fulbright-Hays scholar in Poland. The Russian Institute at Columbia University supported my early efforts to write this book, and the Russian and East European Center at the University of Illinois has been particularly generous in making its resources available to me over the past decade. A variety of grants and other sorts of support from the American Council of Learned Societies, the American Philosophical Society, and the Northern Illinois University Graduate School Fund have rounded out the generous support I have received over the years.

Even the best efforts of family, colleagues, friends, and generous research organizations cannot help a scholar in his work unless libraries and archives make their resources available to him. In this respect, I have been more than fortunate. Serafima Grigorev'na Sakharova at the Central State Historical Archive in Leningrad has placed her awesome knowledge of nineteenth-century archival materials at my disposal over the years, and my debt to her is very great indeed. In the Soviet Union, many other archivists and librarians at the Central State Historical Library, the Lenin Library (and its manuscript section), the Archive of the October Revolution, the Saltykov-Shchedrin Public Library (and its manuscript section), the Archive of the Academy of Sciences, the State

Acknowledgments

Historical Archive of Leningrad Region, the State Historical Museum, Pushkinskii Dom, the Archive of the All-Union Geographical Society, and the Central State Archive of Literature and Art have been generous in their help. They, and their counterparts at the Central Archive of Ancient Acts and the University Library in Warsaw, the British Museum, the Public Record Office, the Archive of Russian and East European History and Culture at Columbia University, the Regenstein Library at the University of Chicago, and the Founders Memorial Library at Northern Illinois University, must remain the unsung heroes in the lengthy tale of the research that went into this book.

As helpful as these many people have been, I must acknowledge yet a further debt to Rebecca Atack, Marianna Tax Choldin, Laurence Miller, Frankie Mosborg, and June Pachuta at the University of Illinois Library for their efforts on my behalf and for the dedication and good humor with which they always met my sometimes outrageous requests for assistance. To them, and to many others in the United States, England, Poland, and the Soviet Union, I owe a special debt that formal thanks such as these cannot begin to repay.

Note on Transliteration

With a few exceptions, the transliteration that I have used in this book follows the Library of Congress system. I have transliterated most names of foreign origin (including Baltic German) directly, without converting them to their national counterparts. The only exceptions to this rule have been the names of foreigners who lived for a time in Russia but did not become Russian citizens. According to the usual practice, all dates are given according to the Julian calendar which, in the nineteenth century, was twelve days behind the Gregorian calendar used in the West.

In the

Vanguard of Reform

ChapTER I

Russia's Bureaucratic World, 1825-1855

"Bureaucratic formalities have reached the point of absurdity."

Count Perovskii

Some months after the death of Nicholas I, a desperate and bitter Russian official complained that "the most distinctive features [of our state administration] consist of a universal lack of truth, the government's distrust of its own instruments, and its contempt for all others." The author of this indictment was P. A. Valuev, Governor of the Baltic province of Courland and soon to become one of Imperial Russia's most effective Ministers of Internal Affairs. Valuev saw the extreme centralization of the Russian bureaucracy and the increasingly mechanistic nature of its administrative processes as two further obstacles that the civil service posed to effective government in Russia. Form, not content, had become his colleagues' chief concern. "All government agencies," he lamented, "are more occupied with each other nowadays than with the substance of those matters for which they are responsible."[1]

Russians long had cursed their civil officials' unyielding devotion to rigid procedures, and Valuev's caustic remarks were unusual only in that they came from the pen of a man who stood near the apex of the Imperial establishment and were circulated widely among the nobility and intelligentsia of St. Petersburg. Still, devotion to the bureaucratic ideals of form and procedure are common in any administration, and the Russian bureaucracy was not dramatically different in that respect from a number of others. For Russians, their officials' unfortunate dedication to these universal bureaucratic traits was made worse during the re-

1

tury before Nicholas I ascended the throne because so many of those who labored in the Tsar's service were poorly educated and understood only imperfectly the problems that confronted them. As we can best determine, less than one out of every five Russian civil servants in 1755 had any formal schooling, and the home educations that many of the remainder received from haphazardly trained tutors often were very poor indeed. By the middle of the eighteenth century, a full forty percent of the men who headed St. Petersburg's central administrative colleges still had no formal education, and only four of their twelve deputies ever had been to school. By comparison with their European counterparts, the educational achievements of the Russians were little short of wretched, but the sad truth was that Russia's rulers could expect little better from even their senior officials because the number of institutions able to provide education beyond the elementary level literally could be counted on the fingers of two hands. Russia's first university was founded only in 1755, and its graduates did not begin to reach the higher echelons of the civil service in noticeable numbers until after the turn of the century.[2]

While the bureaucracy remained relatively small, and the problems facing it reasonably uncomplex, Russia's rulers could rely on special civil and military agents to carry their orders into the provinces and bypass many of the obstacles that a poorly educated, uncompromising, and venal bureaucracy posed to the administration of such far-flung domains as theirs. The use of civic and military agents was a time-honored practice, used ever since Muscovite times, and it continued to be reasonably effective in the hands of officials who still were guided by Muscovite administrative traditions and precedents.[3] Above all, it enabled them to circumvent an otherwise deadly administrative dilemma in which, as Professors Pintner and Rowney recently concluded, "the most talented and best-trained" officials had to rely on "the least educated and least ambitious to execute their policies throughout the realm."[4]

The origins of this dilemma lay in the reforms of Peter the Great. Peter had imposed different imperatives upon his central administration than had his seventeenth-century predecessors, and he had endeavored to alter the structure and organization of the administration to meet his new demands more predictably and efficiently. He therefore had established a more rational institutional structure for Russia's administration by creating the Ruling Senate in 1711 and by founding a series of collegial executive institutions (*kollegii*) between 1718 and 1720. Headed by a board of between ten and thirteen tsarist appointees, each administrative college became responsible for a particular functional area of Russia's government. Its decisions were to be reached collectively, and its members were to take collective responsibility for them.[5] According to the theories of the seventeenth-century German cameralists from which such collegial administrative principles were derived, this form of government made it possible, in the words of one scholar, for "an absolute ruler who wished to increase his revenue and support a standing army . . . [to] impart a measure of rational organization to a political order that rested on a variety of disparate traditional estates."[6] In theory, it also made it possible to diminish challenges to an absolute ruler's authority. "Simple people are prone to mistake an individual . . . as equal to or above the Tsar," wrote Feofan Prokopovich, Peter's leading churchman and political theorist. "They will not be so led astray by an impersonal, collegial body."[7]

Although Peter could establish a new institutional structure for his newly proclaimed Empire, he could not create a new administrative tradition to guide the manner in which officials served him and his government on a daily basis.[8] Peter's civil officials found it all but impossible to comprehend their Emperor's demands, and they therefore sought refuge in the administrative procedures with which they were comfortable and familiar. Especially because senior officials often had limited administrative experience and were not infrequently incompetent, illiterate, or both,[9] the conduct of official matters usually fell to those lesser officials and clerks who served in their personal chanceries, and these often had direct ties with the seventeenth-century Muscovite administration.[10] As the pre-revolutionary historian A. N. Filippov very properly pointed out, such men "were hardly able to introduce a new spirit into the administration and, especially after Peter the Great, they almost completely failed to create that independent administrative body free from arbitrariness about which Peter and his closest associates had dreamed."[11]

Whatever innovations in the spirit and purpose of administration Peter had endeavored to introduce into Russia's institutions of central government faded very soon after his death.[12] Between 1725 and 1762, and even during the early parts of Catherine II's reign, executive functions in Russia's central administration became the province of Imperial favorites. On those occasions when such men exercised their power collectively, they did so through special supreme bodies that stood outside the institutional framework of Russia's central administration, not through Peter's new executive institutions. Only in the mid-1770s and 1780s did Catherine endeavor to re-establish some form and order in Russia's administration when she realized that her Empire's polyglot institutions and traditions could not respond effectively to the changed conditions in Russia. The most dramatic statement of that fact came from the Pugachev Revolt, which burst out of control in 1773–1774, largely because hopelessly tangled lines of authority and slow-moving bureaucratic communication prevented local authorities from crushing it before it got out of hand.

Catherine knew only too well that as a recognized European Power, her Empire could not tolerate such social and economic dislocations as those that stemmed from Pugachev's Revolt. Clearly, civil peace must be preserved, taxes collected, recruits assembled, and iron ore mined, smelted, and forged into weapons to equip Russia's immense standing army if she were to continue the foreign commitments that her status as a Great Power imposed upon her. Such functions required more efficient institutions and more effective administrative precepts than those that had guided Muscovite and Petrine civil servants. Likewise, as senior Russian officials became acquainted with modern Prussian and French bureaucratic practice and, as at least a handful of them were schooled in the principles of the French Enlightenment and the corresponding *Aufklärung* in Germany, they understood that the pre-modern military and fiscal concerns of Muscovite Tsars conformed poorly to the image of a Great Power that their sovereigns hoped to project. To be sure, Russia's military needs continued greater than ever, but, as a Great Power, she also must exhibit some proper concern for her citizens' welfare.[13] To do so, fifty far-flung provinces, spread over a sixth of the globe's surface, had to be tied effectively to a capital that stood geographically remote from most of the Empire.

To meet these more complex demands, Catherine issued her Statute of November 1, 1775, which eliminated the last vestiges of Muscovite forms in Russia's administration. Perhaps most significant of all, she separated the military from Russia's civil administration for all time, so that never again would the army be used to enforce the Sovereign's decrees and collect revenues, as it had under Peter the Great and his early successors. Catherine placed those tasks into the hands of a systematically organized corps of civil officials who extended the bureaucracy that Peter had established only in St. Petersburg and Moscow into Russia's provincial and district capitals.[14] Yet this achievement also had its negative side because the Empress created her new provincial administration only at the cost of Peter's central government. Catherine's new provincial and district agencies usurped many of the central administration's functions, and, for all practical purposes, all but three of Peter's administrative colleges had ceased to function by the end of the century. As the nineteenth century opened, Russia faced a new institutional crisis of staggering dimensions.[15] Just at the moment when Napoleon was beginning to employ France's more effective bureaucracy to marshal her national resources on an unprecedented scale, Russia found herself without a viable central administration.

4

Thus, perhaps the most pressing problem to confront Alexander I when he ascended the throne in 1801 was the urgent need to reconstruct the partially defunct central administration which his grandmother and father had bequeathed. During the first decade of the new century, the young Emperor and his advisers erected the framework for new ministerial institutions that had the potential for governing Russia more effectively. At least in theory, Russia's central administration became concerned with law and legality, exercised increased monocratic authority over subordinate officials and institutions, and saw as its purpose a more intimate and pervasive involvement in the daily lives of the Emperor's subjects.[16] The new ministerial institutions that were to express these broader new concerns were created by the Manifesto of September 8, 1802, which at first did little more than regroup Peter the Great's administrative colleges under the direction of individual ministers rather than resurrect them under the headship of Petrine collegial boards. It was a modest beginning, but from it evolved an administrative apparatus that eventually grew powerful enough to erode the unlimited and undivided power of the autocracy itself.

If Alexander's newly appointed ministers were to wield monocratic authority effectively, they needed at their command officials who could function as true Imperial administrators rather than as defenders of that pre-modern tradition that conditioned the attitudes of most Russian civil servants at the time. As early as 1802, Alexander's brilliant adviser, the great bureaucratic reformer Mikhail Speranskii, insisted that officials be properly educated, not merely trained on the job, and that allegiance to the interests of the state must precede class loyalty in their official duties.[17] Perhaps more obvious than anything else, the administrative difficulties posed by the vast national mobilization of men and resources that Alexander ordered in 1806 showed the validity of Speranskii's argument. Clearly, if Catherine's earlier effort to transfer from the army to the civil service the critical duties of collecting revenue and enforcing the sovereign's will in the provinces was to succeed, if the state was to serve its citizens' welfare, and if these functions were to be coordinated at the center of the government by Alexander's newly appointed ministers, it was essential to have better-educated officials who understood Russia's broader needs and interests.

A search for such officials, and the means to ensure a regular and continuing flow of them into the bureaucracy, occupied progressive Russian statesmen for the next half-century, and their failure to solve that problem became a major element in the Empire's increasing backwardness as mid-century approached. Officials who did not comprehend the broader issues facing Russia, or who defined them primarily

5

in terms of narrow aristocratic self-interest, could not serve as effective instruments for confronting those complex policy issues that centered on Russia's changing economic and social life, even in the limited manner advocated by Nicholas I and some of his closest counselors. Like their eighteenth-century predecessors, such officials hastily withdrew behind that screen of excessive formalism which, for so long, had offered refuge for men who were unwilling, unable, or unprepared to confront those new and complex questions of administration and policy posed by a world in which the tempo of change accelerated at an ever-increasing pace. Inevitably, such an adoration of bureaucratic formalities fed upon itself to generate yet more of the same. As Russia reached mid-century, Minister of Internal Affairs Perovskii had good reason to lament that "it is impossible not to recognize that bureaucratic formalities have reached the point of absurdity."[18] In the words of one of his junior colleagues, these years, the era of Nicholas I, marked "the heyday of formalism."[19]

"The Heyday of Formalism"

Like all bureaucracies, that which functioned in Russia during the second quarter of the nineteenth century was slow, inefficient, and flawed in many ways. Nonetheless, and again like other bureaucracies, it somehow muddled through, and the one indisputable fact was that the Russian Empire continued to function. But there were fundamental differences between the bureaucracies of Russia and Europe. Most particularly, the bureaucratic systems in the West did not act to impede national development when European nations began to enter the Industrial Age. If Russia was to meet the challenge posed by the rapidly industrializing West, she, in turn, had to find some way to achieve greater administrative efficiency and instill into her middle- and upper-level officials a measure of support for change. Russia's bureaucrats had to become responsive to the needs of the nation they served, and some means had to be found to enable those few who were well informed about complex social and economic issues to gain input into the tsarist policy-making process.

Yet the very nature of autocracy worked against the development of impersonal policy-making instruments such as had evolved in the bureaucracies of western Europe. Although Paul I's Fundamental Laws decreed that "the Russian Empire is administered on the bases of absolute laws, regulations, and statutes," they also decreed that all laws "originate with the Autocratic Power." The Emperor was "an Autocratic and Absolute Monarch [and] submission to his supreme authority must come not from fear alone but as a matter of conscience."[20] Coupled with these notions of their absolute power, the preservation of the Romanov dynasty became a fundamental mission of nineteenth-century Emperors, and that dynastic mission stood in opposition to the ideal of a state administered by impersonal institutions "on the bases of absolute laws, regulations, and statutes."[21] The autocrat remained the ultimate source of justice, law, mercy, and many types of privilege, and as Russia entered the post-Napoleonic era, the Emperor, not his ministers, formulated policy. As a result, just when the new social and economic groups that comprised the middle class were eroding the power of absolutism in the West, it was strengthened in Russia.

The obvious dichotomy between impersonal institutions and the Autocrat's personal power had, in fact, been expressed in the Manifesto of September 1802, which replaced Peter the Great's administrative colleges with ministries, for its authors clearly viewed the ministers as the Emperor's personal agents entrusted with certain commissions (*poruchenii*) or administrative responsibilities.[22] The more militaristic order instituted by Nicholas I intensified that view, for he regarded himself as Russia's "commander" and his ministers as his adjutants in a much stronger sense than had his elder brother.[23] He stated that view most dramatically when he designated Minister of State Domains P. D. Kiselev as his "Chief of Staff for Peasant Affairs,"[24] but it applied to all who served him in ministerial capacities. Such minister-adjutants could undertake specific commissions and perform routine tasks, but, just as a military commander insists on holding responsibility for command decisions in his hands, so Nicholas preserved control over each and every policy-making decision in Russia's central administration. Because he insisted on imposing a military command structure upon Russia's central administration, Nicholas thus preferred men who shared his view that "all human life is nothing more than service"[25] to those known for their expert knowledge and technical expertise, especially because such talents tended to be found in men who also had a taste for independent thought.

Nicholas was further encouraged to prefer the service of men over institutions by his association with the historian and conservative ideologist N. M. Karamzin, who was perhaps his closest adviser during the first weeks of his reign. Many of the historian's political views coincided so closely with the young Emperor's own that it appears Nicholas even wanted to appoint Karamzin, a recognized foe of Alexander's new ministerial institutions, to a ministerial post.[26] Karamzin had exhorted Alexander to pay "more attention to men than to forms," to remember that "one of the worst political evils of our time is the absence of fear" and that "skill in choosing and handling men is foremost among

7

the skills that a Russian sovereign must possess."[27] Such sentiments appealed to Nicholas, who had heard similar injunctions from his mother and his tutors throughout his youth.[28] On occasion his elder brother had expressed a preference for administration by institutions, but Nicholas always placed his confidence in men, even as Alexander's ministries continued to develop as the key administrative institutions in Russia.

As might be expected in an autocratic state, it took only a short time before Nicholas's assumption that ministers of state were mere adjutants extended downward throughout the Russian bureaucracy to the relations between senior officials and their subordinates. During the second quarter of the nineteenth century, Russia's central administration saw a dramatic increase in the number of agents of special commissions (*chinovniki osobykh poruchenii*) under the direct control of ministers or their subordinate department heads. According to the "temporary" Tables of Organization (*shtaty*) of the Ministry of Internal Affairs issued in December 1834, there were only twenty such agents in the entire ministry.[29] A mere decade later, ten were assigned to Nikolai Miliutin's Provisional Section for the Reorganization of Municipal Government and Economy in the Ministry's Economic Department alone.[30] Such agents did not serve as mere bureaucratic adjuncts, nor were their positions sinecures for well-born lords who wished to be in service but not to serve. They comprised a vital part of Russia's ministerial administration because they acted as direct extensions of their superiors' authority, and many of those who emerged as enlightened bureaucrats in the 1850s served in such capacities at some point in their careers. Indeed, service as agents of special commissions became an important factor in helping such men to achieve the visibility they needed to rise to higher positions in the bureaucracy.[31]

Nicholas knew that the bureaucratic instruments he had inherited posed serious obstacles to the implementation of policy in his far-flung domains. Yet his efforts to improve them were neither bold nor broadly conceived. His first inclination was to make the bureaucracy more responsive to his will by relying upon minister-adjutants chosen from his circle of closest friends. Very quickly he increased their numbers by establishing the Third Section of His Majesty's Own Chancery, an entire corps of adjutants established to serve as extensions of his autocratic *persona* throughout Russia. Although their numbers increased, all of Nicholas's adjutants found their spheres of activity severely circumscribed by their Emperor's narrow perception of the bureaucracy's flaws and his limited understanding about how such might be remedied. Perhaps Speranskii stated this view most clearly when he endeavored to define the responsibilities of a special committee that Nicholas had established on December 6, 1826. The Committee of December 6th was to examine Russia's administration and comment on the social and political problems it faced, but Speranskii insisted that its task could not be "the full alteration of the existing order of government, but only its refinement by means of a few particular changes and additions."[32] Nicholas never questioned the functions of Russia's ministries and administrative departments. He merely insisted on further regulation and pressed for more precise information about how his Empire's administration functioned under the adjutants he had put into key positions. Therefore, it was no accident that Russia's government agencies kept better statistical data during the reign of Nicholas I than they did during the 1860s and 1870s. That was the only way in which they could respond to the Emperor's efforts to define more precisely their tasks and relationships to each other.[33]

Nicholas's misplaced confidence that properly chosen adjutants could implement his will throughout his domains was probably best reflected in Mikhail Pogodin's joyous reassurances to Russia's reading public that "one educated, zealous, active superior—and the entire department entrusted to him is . . . aiding other departments by its example, organization and training of officials. One governor with such qualities—and one fiftieth part of Russia is prospering."[34] Nicholas endeavored to find just such men for top posts in his government, and he encouraged them to recruit others to serve under them. But, he emphasized the virtues of zealous service at the expense of education and thoughtful planning, with the result that Russia's central bureaucracy dissipated its resources by a show of frenzied activity that served no worthwhile purpose and produced few results. It became more important to appear busy than to become seriously concerned about vital issues of state policy. "Always say that you are occupied, but do not explain the nature of your work," wrote one senior official in a satirical commentary about bureaucratic life. "Let people think your work is part of a secret inquiry. That way, people will think that you are involved with important state affairs."[35]

Emphasis on zealous service and the quantity of reports and communications that each department generated encouraged the production of documents (the process known in Russian as *deloproizvodstvo*) to flourish unrestrained by any limitations of common sense. The quantity of reports written, and the number of official cases processed, became measures of each agency's achievement and figured prominently in its annual report.[36] As Minister of Internal Affairs Lev Perovskii so aptly put it, Russia's civil servants had become mere "record-keepers,"[37] who engaged in what one frustrated young official called "a lot of arguments and passing official papers from hand to hand."[38] The question of making policy slipped further out of focus as harassed senior officials struggled to deal with the flood of petty administrative tasks they faced every day. Each year, frantic provincial governors confronted an appalling mountain of more than 100,000 documents that required their signatures,[39] and senior statesmen in St. Petersburg were no less pressed. Once established, this ubiquitous routine of wasting statesmen's time on administrative detail persevered. Writing in the 1870s, Russia's then-retired Minister of Public Instruction A. V. Golovnin complained that petty bureaucratic tasks still prevented statesmen from giving their best attention to the serious business of government:

> From conversations with our present-day statesmen [Golovnin wrote], it is evident that, because of the vast quantity of matters of secondary importance ... [and because of] their Court and social obligations, they have absolutely no opportunity ... to reflect upon things, and to gain some perspective upon the general state of affairs, the general course of legislation, and the nature of our administrative activities in general.[40]

Perpetuation of the bureaucratic process, not the serious tasks of policy-making and creative administration, thus consumed the time of Russia's statesmen and sapped their energies. Much was talked about, but little was accomplished. "We go one step forward and take two steps backward, and we shall not get very far in this manner," wrote one amazed newcomer to the St. Petersburg bureaucracy at mid-century. "Today, we say: 'Excellent!' 'Let's do this!' But tomorrow, we shall say, 'Yes, this is fine to be sure ... but it can wait.' And then we shall turn to a new matter altogether."[41] The Emperor and his closest advisers might believe that men, not institutions, could produce the most effective administration, but men overwhelmed by regulations and trivial daily tasks simply could never get the forest into focus because they were obliged to spend all their time pruning and cultivating each tree. That problem was made even worse because there were so few officials who were well enough educated to even comprehend the forest's dimensions. As had been the case since the days of Peter the Great, the issue of education continued to assume critical importance.

Although the demand for better educated, better trained civil officials never was satisfied during the first half of the nineteenth century, at least some statesmen tried to find ways to meet it. Soon after it was established in 1802, Alexander I's new Ministry of Public Instruction prepared grandiose plans for increasing the number of district schools, provincial *gimnazii,* and universities in Russia. Even though the entire scheme never was realized, the first two decades of the century saw universities established at Vilna, Dorpat, Kharkov, Kazan, and St. Petersburg.[42] Perhaps most significant of all, in 1811, Alexander founded a lyceum at Tsarskoe Selo for the avowed purpose of "educating those youths especially destined for important spheres of state service."[43] The Lyceum was to provide an elite education for aristocratic youths who planned careers in Russia's service, and its graduates were promised the same service grades as young men who completed the course at the university. At Speranskii's urging, Alexander insisted that the Lyceum develop a progressive curriculum to educate students in those areas needed by nineteenth-century administrators.[44]

Alexander I, Speranskii, and those statesmen who supported their efforts to develop Russia's educational facilities first had to convince the sons of nobles to abandon casual study with tutors and submit to the rigidity of a formal curriculum at the Empire's new schools and universities. With the Emperor's personal sponsorship, and its elite student body, the Tsarskoe Selo Lyceum attracted, from the very beginning, its full complement of talented students, but the new *gimnazii* and universities remained only partly filled, despite an ominous paragraph in the Decree on the Establishment of Schools (January 29, 1803) which warned that after five years, "no one who has failed to graduate from a public or private secondary school will be admitted to the civil service in posts requiring juridical or other specialized knowledge."[45]

Although at first there was some room to argue about which posts in the civil service required "other specialized knowledge" and which did not, the Emperor removed all cause for doubt in 1809 when, in consultation with his closest advisers, he made good on the warning he had issued in 1803. After noting that most schools were still short of students and that Russia's civil administration required far more educated officials than were graduating from the Empire's schools, Alexander decreed on August 6th that no official could be promoted to the rank of *kollezhskii asessor* (grade eight, which conferred lifetime nobility) unless he had graduated from a university or an elite school, such as the Tsarskoe Selo Lyceum, or passed an examination judged to measure university level education. For officials who already held grades eight through six, their path toward the coveted rank of *statskii sovetnik* (grade five, which conferred hereditary nobility) was barred unless they met the same requirements.[46]

This decree engendered bitterness among a substantial number of Russian bureaucrats. Nikolai Karamzin, the Empire's official historian and self-appointed spokesman for the nobility, complained that:

> In Russia, the official presiding in the Civil Court must know Homer and Theocritus, the Senate Secretary—the properties of

oxygen and all the gasses, the Deputy Governor—Pythagorean geometry, the superintendent of a lunatic asylum—Roman law, or else they will end their days as Collegiate and Titular counsellors [the ranks immediately below those of *statskii sovetnik* and *kollezh-skii asessor* in the Table of Ranks]. Neither forty years of state service, nor important accomplishments exempt one from the obligation of having to learn things which are entirely alien and useless for Russians.[47]

Of course, the law was not always applied stringently, and, in 1834, it was changed so that an official's lack of higher education merely slowed his rise but did not halt it.[48] Nevertheless, even before Nicholas I ascended the throne in 1825, it had become clear that the Russian Emperor required better educated officals than were generally available to staff the middle levels of his civil service.

A shortage of officials sufficiently well educated to confront increasingly complex social, economic, and technological issues was only one of the serious problems that plagued Russia's administration in the post-Napoleonic era. More generally, and setting aside the issue of the provincial bureaucracy's many faults, which cannot concern us here, Nicholas I and his senior advisers simply did not have at their disposal a corps of officials who could supply them with accurate information about the social, economic, or political conditions in the Empire at any given time. Although the bureaucracy had achieved a minimal level of semi-literacy, it had not yet become the sort of instrument that Nicholas and his confidants required to resolve the problems that Russia faced in the 1830s and 1840s.

During the first half of the nineteenth century, and especially as its mid-point neared, the Russian bureaucracy grew from a relatively compact corps of noble officials assisted by a few near-proletarian scribes into a more ponderous administrative body that was even less responsive to the autocrat's will than its eighteenth-century predecessor had been. In terms of raw numbers, personnel in the Table of Ranks increased from approximately 16,000 in 1796 to 75,201 in 1850, while the Empire's population increased from approximately 36 to 69 million.[49] Thus, in the space of fifty years, the number of civil officials burgeoned by an astounding 470 percent while the population they served did not quite double. Although it has been argued that the tsarist administration employed only a quarter as many civil servants in proportion to Russia's inhabitants as did its counterparts in France and England,[50] the fact remains that a third of the Empire's population never saw a government official from one decade to the next. Throughout the first half of the nineteenth century, the Empire's serf-owners or their bailiffs collected taxes, assembled recruits, and administered justice to the 22 million men and women who tilled their estates. Only Russia's nobles and townsfolk dealt with state officials in the manner of English and French citizens, and state peasants (the largest single group in the Empire) encountered them far less frequently.

The economic disruption and social dislocation caused by the Napoleonic wars, coupled with Alexander I's neglect of domestic affairs during the last decade of his reign, meant that much of the rapid growth in Russia's bureaucracy occurred during the reign of Nicholas I. Yet the significant influx of new officials into the civil service did not mean that increased numbers of men and women came to know the relative comfort and prestige enjoyed by numbers of Catherinian civil servants a half-century before. Throughout the first half of the nineteenth century, tsarist statesmen treated the rank and file in Russia's army of civil servants as a sort of clerical proletariat whose ranks were swollen further by thousands of chancery copyists who had not yet reached even the lowest grade in the Table of Ranks. The numbers of these so-called *kantseliarskie sluzhiteli* increased from 26,377 in 1850 (the first year for which figures are available) to 32,073 in 1857, although their ratio to the civil servants holding grades in the Table of Ranks generally remained quite constant.[51] Clearly, such men were at the bottom of the civil service pyramid, and it was rare for one of them to rise very far into the Table of Ranks. In fact, Valuev was one of a mere handful of civil servants to rise to high office in nineteenth-century Russia after entering the bureaucracy as a humble *kantseliarskii sluzhitel'*.

In 1845, a decade before he penned his well-known indictment of Russia's civil administration, Valuev confided his thoughts about the aspirations of middle-level civil servants to a memorandum that he addressed to Minister of Internal Affairs L. A. Perovskii. By that time he already had become a *kollezhskii asessor* and had enjoyed for more than three years the privileges of lifetime nobility that his rank conferred. Perovskii had just attached him to General E. A. Golovin, Governor-General of Riga, as an official of special commissions on an assignment that earned him three extraordinarily rapid promotions so that by January 1850, more than nine months before his thirty-fourth birthday, Valuev had won hereditary noble status.[52] "Everyone knows that the lower official grades are only a Purgatory through which runs the measured highway to the paradise of delights [i.e. the rank of *statskii sovetnik*] for those who are ambitious,"[53] Valuev wrote from this vantage point as a highly successful civil servant. His comment summarized the goal of every ambitious junior official in the Empire. The more serious question was how many such men had a reasonable hope of realizing that aspiration.

No one would dispute that promotion to the rank that carried with it hereditary noble status was ardently sought by junior civil servants in Russia, but its attainment usually was an arduous undertaking. The Civil Service Statute of May 1834 divided officials into three categories *(razriady)* based on their level of formal education, and each category had a different schedule of promotions for time served in grade *(za vyslugu let)*.[54] It took an official in the first category twenty-four years to rise from the rank of *kollezhskii registrator* (grade fourteen) to that of *statskii sovetnik* (grade five) by means of promotions for time served in grade, while it required thirty years for officials in the second category, and thirty-seven years for those in the third. These promotion schedules were lengthened for officials who were not of noble birth, so that it required twenty-six, thirty-six, and forty-two years for first, second, and third category plebian officials to reach the rank of *statskii sovetnik* if all their promotions were for time served in grade and came on time.[55]

Even though officials were eligible for time-in-grade promotions after a specified number of years, that did not guarantee that promotions would come on schedule. At mid-century, the portion of officials in the Table of Ranks who received promotions each year ranged between only six and ten percent, although most promotions below the rank of *statskii sovetnik* required no more than four years of service in grade. Because considerably more civil servants were eligible for time-in-grade promotions than the number who received them, there was no certainty that an official could, in fact, reach the coveted rank of *statskii sovetnik* before middle age or, even, before retirement, though it was theoretically possible to do so according to Russia's civil service statutes.

This arduous promotion schedule could be shortened if an ambitious official could win promotions for merit *(za otlichie)* rather than wait to be advanced for time served in grade. In that way, an official in the first category could reach grade five from grade fourteen in the space of fifteen, not twenty-four, years, while his counterparts in the second category could do so in twenty-two, and those in the third in twenty-six years. For civil servants with elite or university educations, who often entered the bureaucracy at grades nine or ten, it became possible to reach hereditary noble status in as little as nine years, or before they reached the age of thirty.[56] To be eligible for such promotions, they needed to accomplish "some particular achievement on behalf of the service in administrative affairs, or demonstrate particular merit and achievement as an official."[57] One might expect that in a country where the Emperor preferred senior officials who were "not so much wise as service-oriented,"[58] and where he valued service longevity in making high-level appointments,[59] promotions for merit would have been relatively rare, but they came frequently enough, in fact, to encourage

14

ambitious young men to strive for them. Between 1847 and 1857 (the only decade during the first half of the nineteenth century for which we have information), the percentage of promotions for merit ranged between six and eighteen percent of the total. Certainly that was sufficient to give some encouragement to that minority of truly ambitious young men who entered the Table of Ranks at its lower levels, and a number of prominent statesmen of the 1860s and 1870s built their careers in just such a fashion.[60]

Of course advancement in the Russian bureaucracy was a considerably more complex matter than such raw statistical data indicate, and promotions for merit did not hinge only upon "some particular achievement in administrative affairs on behalf of the service" or "particular merit and achievement as an official." It was so well known to nineteenth-century Russians, for example, that an ambitious official could advance rapidly if he won the patronage of a high-ranking statesman that this became a recurring theme in the letters, diaries, even the *belles lettres,* of the period. "By the fortunate chance of drawing attention to oneself by a clever trick or by successful flattery, the careers of many [officials] in Russia are advanced," wrote one young army officer who had just come to St. Petersburg in the mid-1840s.[61] S. I. Zarudnyi, later to play an important part in drafting the Judicial Reform Statute of 1864, put the matter even more bluntly in a satirical essay when he concluded that, "if you have patronage, you will be considered a genius, able to undertake any task, and you will advance rapidly. But, if you do not have patronage, then you will be considered an utter fool, fit for nothing, and knowing nothing."[62]

Data for the mid-century make it clear that promotions for merit came far more frequently in certain agencies and that ambitious young civil servants obviously had better opportunities to advance their careers in some ministries than in others. At the top of the scale stood a group of elite ministries and central directorates where advancements for merit accounted for between thirty-five and one hundred percent of all promotions granted. These included (in descending order) the State Secretariat for the Affairs of the Grand Duchy of Finland (100%), the Chancery of the Committee of Ministers (51.5%), the Commission on Petitions (48.6%), the State Chancery (48.14%), His Majesty's Own Chancery (41.7%), the Ministry of Foreign Affairs (40.1%), and the State Secretariat for Polish Affairs (35.7%). Men who served in these agencies clearly comprised a privileged group, and their careers usually advanced rapidly, according to an elite pattern.

Below those elite agencies in which positions were obtained particularly as a consequence of birth or high influence stood a second group of ministries and directorates where merit promotions accounted for between twelve and seventeen percent of the total. These were the Ministry of State Domains (16.8%), the Office of the State Comptroller (14.7%), the Ministry of Internal Affairs (14.2%), and the Ministry of Justice (12.4%). Actually, the percentage of merit promotions for officials serving in the central offices of the Ministries of Internal Affairs, Justice, and State Domains must have been considerably greater than these raw data indicate because a very large portion of these agencies' personnel served in the provinces, where chances for merit promotions were very limited. Indeed, according to the annual reports of the *Inspektorskii Departament,* only 4.3% of the officials in the Ministry of Internal Affairs, 14.9% of the officials in the Ministry of Justice, and 22.5% of the officials in the Ministry of State Domains served in St. Petersburg, and it was they who received most of the promotions for merit.[63]

In Russia's remaining ministries, the portion of merit promotions was below ten percent. Clearly, these were not the agencies in which an energetic and ambitious young official would choose to serve, for in these, merit seems to have been rewarded only in rare instances.[64] Most important for our purposes, that fact seems to have led those young, ambitious officials who emerged as Russia's enlightened bureaucrats at mid-century to seek positions in the Ministries of Internal Affairs, State Domains, and Justice. Those who were less aggressive or less competent were content to allow their careers to advance more slowly by promotions for time served in grade in such agencies as the Ministry of Public Instruction, the Postal Department, and the Directorate of Roads and Public Buildings. Probably it is not mere coincidence that no cadres of enlightened bureaucrats emerged from those ministries in which seniority played the central role in career advancement.

In whatever ministry they were employed, and wherever they served in the Russian Empire, ambitious civil servants aspired to serve in the chanceries of the capital and, once they obtained a position, to remain there at all costs. St. Petersburg was the Empire's cultural center, and Russians served there to be near the heart of its cultural life as well as to be close to the glittering and opulent world of the Imperial family, prominent statesmen, and famous courtiers. The great brick and stone buildings of Peter's northern capital, their tall glass windows staring out upon wide avenues and canals, the city's cleanliness in comparison to other Russian urban centers, the rich array of goods in its shops, the elegant equipages that rolled along its boulevards, and, perhaps most of all, the chance of encountering some great lord, statesman, or even the Emperor in the street made St. Petersburg a fascinating place for newly arrived provincials.[65]

Besides these tangible attractions, Russia's capital exerted an almost magnetic pull upon men born and educated in the provinces, as M. E. Saltykov-Shchedrin, himself a civil servant of some considerable experience in St. Petersburg, later explained in his *Diary of a Provincial in St. Petersburg:*

> We provincials [he wrote] somehow turn our steps toward Petersburg instinctively. We may sit at home for days and months on end—and suddenly, we begin to move. . . . A person will be sitting around and suddenly, as if a light had dawned, he begins to pack his things. "You're going to Petersburg?"—"To Petersburg!" he replies. And that says all that needs to be said. It is as if Petersburg, all by itself, with its name, its streets, its fog, rain, and snow, could resolve something or shed some new light on something.[66]

Some years after he had come to the capital to serve in the Ministry of Internal Affairs' chancery, A. I. Artem'ev, a young statistician from Kazan, thought in similar terms when he confided to his diary that "I still do not understand very clearly why I came to St. Petersburg, for I had not one single acquaintance among the city's half-million inhabitants . . . and absolutely no patron whatsoever."[67] Again, it was the dream that radiated from Russia's great capital, the city so unlike any other in the Empire, that drew Artem'ev and the people Saltykov-Shchedrin described to it. Like most provincial Russians, they expected something new, different, and somehow better to happen in their lives once they reached it. At first, they were caught up in its magical aura, in that illusion which the novelist Nikolai Gogol, himself a provincial who had come to the capital, characterized so vividly in his early stories. "O, do not trust the Nevskii Prospekt!" he warned the readers of his tale that bore the great avenue's name. "Everything's an illusion. Everything's a dream. Everything's not what it seems!"[68]

For young civil servants who sought to make their way in St. Petersburg, the most illusory phantom of all was success itself. Artem'ev's retrospective wonderment at his youthful audacity in coming to the capital when he had no patron is especially understandable because patronage was doubly important to the success of any young man's career in St. Petersburg. So important was a patron's support that young Ivan Roskovshenko, who came to St. Petersburg from Kiev in 1831, went immediately to buy cloth for a new suit so that he would make the proper impression on those who might start him on his way. "I cannot yet appear before any of my future patrons," he lamented to a friend as he searched frantically for a way to earn enough to pay the tailor and collect his new clothes.[69]

Most would-be civil servants did not share Roskovshenko's good fortune to have the names of several senior officials to call on. Most had no patron and knew no influential men. Some carried deep within an inner pocket a precious slip of paper that bore the name of some third-hand acquaintance—a friend of a friend of a distant relative, perhaps—who, they hoped, might offer guidance or, perhaps, even a much-needed introduction. Failure was common. Many never found a position because even graduation from an elite school did not guarantee them a place in the bureaucracy. Graduation only conferred upon them the privilege of entering the civil service at a certain rank when, or if, they found a vacancy. Sometimes, fortuitous accident aided their search, as in the case of young Konstantin Veselovskii, who graduated first in his class at the Lyceum at Tsarskoe Selo and later became a noted member of the Imperial Academy of Sciences.

> One fine day in the fall of 1838 [Veselovskii recalled many years later], I found myself in the streets of St. Petersburg, all alone as if in a forest. I had no patrons and no useful acquaintances; there was not even anyone to offer advice. My entire circle of acquaintances was limited to my comrades from the Lyceum, who were just as inexperienced in practical matters as was I. . . . Knowing from gossip just how difficult it was to find a position without a patron's support . . . I decided that I stood a better chance in the . . . only recently established Ministry of State Domains, in which the right of occupying vacant positions could not as yet have been established by seniority.[70]

That a winner of the first-place gold medal in the Lyceum's final examinations should find himself in such a position after he had graduated from the school whose avowed purpose was to train future Russian statesmen was one of countless absurd situations that plagued the Russian bureaucracy in those years. Even more absurd, when they found a position, such talented young men needed a patron to raise them above the anonymous mass of low-ranking officials that filled St. Petersburg's chanceries. There is no way to determine even approximately how much talent was lost to the Russian government because men of ability failed to find positions or did not win the attention of some senior official. Certainly, the loss may have been considerable, and it was openly regretted by at least one of the progressive statesmen who served Alexander II during the Great Reform Era.[71]

Added to the difficulties of finding positions and patrons, the exorbitant cost of living in St. Petersburg was the most ubiquitous problem that civil servants faced. During the 1830s and 1840s, the most modest lodgings cost from ten to fifteen silver rubles a month, so that even if several shared a small flat, the cost to each still was high.[72] Food consumed an equally large portion of the young officials' meager salaries because lodgings which rented for under twenty rubles a month usually had no kitchens. Many young officials took their meals in inexpensive eating houses (kukhmisterskie), but the cost of approximately seven silver rubles a month was so high that three junior civil servants often pooled their resources to purchase two monthly meal tickets and then shared the meals. Those who could not afford even that sum took their meals with private families whose poverty made them willing to share their humble fare with strangers in return for the few kopeks they received for meals that were neither nourishing nor palatable.[73]

Throughout the Nicholas era, tsarist statesmen treated the rank and file civil officials who staffed Russia's government offices as a sort of clerical proletariat who were not expected to live comfortably or even decently. To understand better the burden that St. Petersburg's high cost of living placed on this growing army of impoverished civil servants, we should look for a moment at the salaries they received. According to the surprisingly accurate records maintained by the *Inspektorskii Departament*, which functioned as a sort of oversight bureau for the civil service during the last decade of Nicholas's reign, almost ninety percent of Russia's officials received salaries that were too low to provide even a modest standard of living. In 1847, the average monthly salary earned by St. Petersburg civil servants (including food and housing allowances for which many lesser officials did not qualify) was 67.8 rubles. Such a sum hardly seems generous, but it becomes significantly lower when we take into account that such calculations are inflated by the unusually high average monthly salaries (ranging from 120 to 238 rubles) that were paid to officials in His Majesty's Own Chancery, the State Chancery, and the State Secretariats for Polish and Finnish Affairs. Average monthly salaries and allowances in most ministries were well below 67 rubles, and, in the Ministry of Justice, it stood at the truly miserly level of 37 rubles 10 kopeks, a figure that actually declined during the next decade.[74] Lesser officials received well below the average, since it was a fact of life in the Russian bureaucracy that senior statesmen received princely salaries ranging up to as much as 16,000 rubles a year.[75]

Complaints confided to diaries, letters, and memoirs confirm the gloomy picture of penury presented by these impersonal statistics, and it seems that it was not at all unusual for a junior civil servant to earn a monthly salary of less than twenty silver rubles.[76] Of course, poor salaries for young men who were learning a trade or business were the rule in western Europe and the United States at the same time, but it was a premium that many were willing to pay in return for the chance at greater rewards later on. In Russia, young officials could not consider their low salaries as mere poorly paid short-term apprenticeships because many years often passed before their ranks and salaries allowed them even a passable standard of living. The question of wages and prices in St. Petersburg at this time still remains largely unexplored, but the limited evidence suggests that it was not until an official reached the position of *stolonachal'nik* (chief of an office section) that he even had a modest hope of living in moderate comfort.[77] Yet it was more a hope than a certainty, for even a *stolonachal'nik* could not live comfortably on his regular monthly salary of approximately 60 rubles plus food and housing allowances, and it was necessary for him to come close to doubling that income to be assured of a comfortable standard of living.[78]

Officials' pressing need to supplement their salaries made corruption and bribe-taking a certainty. Of course, it is now no secret that many Russian officials thought it no sin to accept bribes as a means to raise their salaries. But it is important to remember that bribes supplemented the salaries mainly of officials whose incomes already were well above the subsistence level, not those for whom even a few additional rubles could have made a critical difference in their way of life, because low-level bureaucrats could provide very little in the way of services. Those who had limited access to bribes, or were perhaps too honest to accept them, had to augment their meager incomes in other ways. Writing for literary, scholarly, and technical journals was a source of income that sustained a number of the progressive young men whose careers, ideas, and political methods we shall examine at greater length in subsequent chapters. It was no accident that the Ministries of State Domains, Public Instruction, and Internal Affairs began to publish official journals during the Nicholas era or that during the 1840s senior officials used these journals as a means to supplement the salaries of talented young bureaucrats who served in their departments. Several of the men who stood in the ranks of the enlightened bureaucrats or were closely associated with them in the 1850s and 1860s used their editorship of these journals as a means for developing effective networks of influence within the central bureaucracy during the 1830s and 1840s.[79]

Drab, poor, and lonely though their lives were, the majority of St. Petersburg's clerkish legions were convinced that their daily labors were worthwhile and important. "I believed so absolutely in the usefulness of such office work," one official recalled, "that each new document we produced seemed to me to be a new current of benevolence flowing from

20

Caricature of a government office, from A. Agin's illustrations of Gogol's Dead Souls

[our office near] Chernyshev Bridge into the vastness of Russia."[80] If such sentiments had expressed a conviction that civil servants were capable of exercising a positive influence on Russian life, they would have been commendable. To Russia's misfortune, they articulated only a groundless faith in the efficacy of bureaucratic measures, and a belief that form and routine in themselves could achieve positive ends. At best it was a misplaced hope; at worst, it perpetuated the myth of Russia's benevolent bureaucracy. "Just look at the annual reports [prepared by each ministry and directorate]," Valuev exclaimed in disgust. "Everywhere, everything possible has been done. Everywhere success has been achieved. Everywhere the prescribed order is being established, if not immediately, then at least gradually. . . . On the surface it all seems splendid, but it is rotting away underneath." It all was part of an attempt, Valuev concluded, to "perpetuate the official lie" that the bureaucracy was working energetically to achieve real and positive benefits for the nation.[81]

Contrary to so many bureaucrats' image of themselves, it probably would not be an overstatement to say that the official who spent a portion of his day working on a matter of some real significance was the exception rather than the rule. At all levels of the central government, civil servants dedicated countless hours to trivial forms and regulations. Even in the State Council, very minor issues—for example, irregularities in the records of a provincial court or the release from service of a minor bureaucrat who had falsified his residence permit—absorbed the attention of high officials who should have thought about far more important matters.[82] Outside the State Council, a single example can illustrate how absurdly time-consuming even the most routine procedures had become during the Nicholas era if we remember that whenever a nobleman put a piece of land up for sale, the bureaucracy at the central and local levels produced at least 1,351 separate documents.[83]

Of course paperwork did not increase in the Russian bureaucracy only because officials hoped to create work with which to occupy their time, although that was a factor. As Minister of Internal Affairs L. A. Perovskii pointed out in one of his reports, a number of regulations and procedures had been implemented during the previous quarter-century in an effort to reduce bureaucrats' despotic treatment of the people they were supposed to serve.[84] This effort had gone too far, Perovskii hastened to add, and the entire administrative process had become burdened by "difficulties resulting from the never-ending increase of official files and papers."[85] By mid-century, files of official papers were piling up in St. Petersburg's chanceries at such a rate that agencies had to establish procedures for destroying them in order to make room for the new ones their officials were producing. "Here in Russia, the most simple and inconsequential matter, which is dealt with by the stroke of a pen elsewhere, generates a whole series of official papers: inquiries, communications, and applications," the noted economist L. V. Tengoborskii wrote in a secret memorandum. "Records and letters seem to reproduce themselves, one might say, in geometrical proportions."[86]

This paper avalanche caused many officials to see administration in terms of producing documents rather than solving important problems.

Most of all, these officials developed mechanistic responses to the situations they confronted, as Mikhail Veselovskii, a young civil servant who found a position in the Petersburg office of the Ministry of Internal Affairs after serving for a number of years in the provinces, later recalled.

> The administrative machine functioned with irreproachable harmony and elegance of detail [he wrote]. Officials believed in the usefulness of their work and loved it for itself alone. It was enough simply to look at the Director of the Department of General Affairs, A. A. Gvodzev, to gain some insight into the quintessence of St. Petersburg's elegant and majestic official world. When he, elegant, freshly shaven, and perfumed, entered the reception chamber . . . and approached those subordinates and petitioners who awaited him, it was impossible to tear one's eyes away from the elastic, undulating movements of his body. Depending on to whom he was speaking, he resembled either the awe-inspiring countenance of Jupiter or the fawning figure of an enchantress seeking to curry favor.[87]

In this world of petitions, applications, inquiries, and reports, the production of documents became an important criterion by which civil servants measured their importance against their rivals. To make certain that senior officials would call on them to prepare important documents, ambitious chancery scribes and junior officials labored to make their handwriting elegant, embellished reports with eye-catching designs, and even on occasion added charts hand-tinted with watercolors.[88] Even the shade of ink was important, and superiors often ordered scribes whose ink was too faint, or who failed to space the lines of the text with absolute precision, to copy documents again and again.[89]

Extreme emphasis upon form over content thus seriously hindered the business of administration in the Russian Empire. Even though he had a hand in creating the problem,[90] Minister of Internal Affairs Perovskii was very candid in pointing out that forms and regulations were beginning to paralyze the bureaucracy. "Endless correspondence absorbs all the attention and energy of men who are supposed to execute policy, and, instead of true supervision and administration, we have, for the most part, only record-keeping and accounting for documents," he reported to the Emperor in 1851.[91] Yet overriding concern with unimportant matters was only part of a larger problem that was made much worse by the central offices' frequent "urgent" requests for information from other agencies. St. Petersburg officials often labeled requests for information as urgent because anything sent through normal channels moved with such glacial slowness that, according to at least one account, even the Emperor had to wait for four or five months for offices in the capital to reply to some of his routine requests.[92] Because each agency had its own prescribed form in which replies to "urgent" requests had to be submitted, each had to be dealt with separately, even though there was a great amount of duplication. Perovskii was amazed to find that his own ministry dealt with more than 165,000 "urgent" requests every year and was even more appalled to learn that a very substantial number were for nothing more than information needed to bring officials' personal service records up to date.[93] Because civil servants had to set all else aside to deal with such "urgent" requests, Perovskii found that questions of real substance and importance sometimes were set aside for years while officials labored to keep abreast of the endless routine matters that flooded into their offices.[94] Even the most diligent efforts to stem this tide seemed doomed. One recent study estimates that as many as 3,300,000 requests and decrees still awaited action in the early 1840s.[95]

Not only was the St. Petersburg bureaucracy slow to respond to requests for information, and even slower to implement new administrative policies, but the accuracy of its reports was marred because officials often reported only what they thought their superiors wanted to hear. Particularly after 1850, when senior bureaucrats received absolute and arbitrary power to remove subordinates from office, lower-ranking civil servants lived in fear of arousing their displeasure and tempered their memoranda accordingly.[96] A. I. Artem'ev admitted as much in 1855, but he confided his frustrations only to the pages of a diary where they remained hidden for more than a century. "If only one line of my lengthy report [about the Old Believers] could be thought of as fully satisfying, deserving of consideration, and persuasive, I would be content," he lamented. "But there are so many misgivings and doubts," he continued. "In all good conscience, I ought not to be silent ... but they [his superiors] can wipe me from the face of the earth. And thus," he confessed, "from necessity, one remains silent."[97] Artem'ev wrote about an area of Russian experience that was sensitive in both political and religious terms, and he obviously felt the need for caution. Yet his fear of reporting accurately the facts that contradicted what his superiors wanted to hear seems to have been the rule, not the exception. Even a decade later, A. V. Golovnin remarked on similar problems at the ministerial level and noted that no one wanted to report bad news to the Emperor for fear of losing his position.[98]

Underpaid, poorly educated officials who were overwhelmed by the endless petty routines that Russia's formalistic bureaucratic system imposed upon them made long-term administration difficult and the chances for effective transformation remote. Yet the myriad and complex problems Russia faced during the Nicholas era needed to be confronted and solutions considered, at least in terms of renovating the existing order, if not its full-fledged reform. There is no need to list here the economic, social, and political difficulties that Russia faced at the time, for these now are well known and often commented upon.[99] But to Russians living during the Nicholas era, the gravity of the problems was far less obvious and the apparent solutions not very complex. Daniel Orlovsky pointed out recently that during the 1860s and 1870s, bureaucratic reformers in the Ministry of Internal Affairs found it "easier to co-opt social groups or institutions into the bureaucratic system they understood best than to identify and eliminate deeper causes of problems."[100] For the senior statesmen who served Nicholas I, the issues at first seemed even less complex, and the problems seemed to have no deeper causes. Convinced as they were that politics lay fully within the realm of administration, and that all political action therefore must be confined within the chanceries of St. Petersburg, these statesmen saw renovation in terms of careful administrative adjustment. In their view, the political instruments of autocracy were well conceived and structurally sound. All that was needed, they thought, was to adjust the machinery of government so that everywhere it would function with that "irreproachable harmony and elegance of detail" that so entranced young Mikhail Veselovskii when he first witnessed the workings of Gvozdev's Department of General Affairs at mid-century. For senior officials of the 1830s and 1840s, the dilemmas Russia faced could best be resolved by adjusting bureaucratic instruments of authority so that they could serve all the functions that their creators had entrusted to them at the beginning of the century.

Adjusting Bureaucratic Instruments of Authority

Not long after Paul I's assassination in 1801, Alexander I's close friend and frequent confidant Count Pavel Stroganov insisted that the superior sensibility and understanding of the Emperor's most intimate advisers should "stand in the same relationship to our body politic as does the art of a physician to the healing of illness."[101] Among Alexander's Young Friends, who formed the so-called "Unofficial Committee" at the beginning of his reign and endeavored to realize Stroganov's vision as Imperial advisers, efforts at administrative reorganization and reform were a response to the political pressures they confronted in the decade after the French Revolution, to the psychological and intellectual crisis that accompanied their rise to power, and to the administrative and institutional dilemmas the Russian state had faced during the last quarter of the eighteenth century. These pressures were intensified by the manner in which they had encountered the ideas of the Enlightenment on the eve of the French Revolution. Close family ties had been absent from their childhood and adolescent experiences, and they had turned to the writings of the late Enlightenment and early sentimentalism in the absence of any traditional environment from which to draw their beliefs and values.[102] From these works they drew their ideals about life, service, and reform. They therefore came to maturity in a European cultural and intellectual world that combined those very elements of middle-class thought and aristocratic life that the French Revolution had so recently proved incompatible.

The views held by Alexander and his Young Friends embodied both authoritarian and libertarian elements, and the authoritarian strand was quickly strengthened at the expense of the libertarian one. Perhaps most important, Paul I's dynastic legislation had proclaimed self-preservation to be a major mission of autocracy, and that set the course which Alexander and his Young Friends chose to follow.[103] Their choice of the authoritarian elements of Enlightenment thought led them to defend autocratic power rather than impose upon it those limits advocated by the teachings of such mentors as the Tsar's famous Swiss tutor LaHarpe, and, in the ministerial reform of 1802, they therefore endeavored to allocate administrative functions to various ministries in a more rational manner without infringing upon the autocrat's power.[104] In contrast to their predecessors in Peter the Great's administrative colleges, ministers were endowed with increased monocratic authority, but it could be exercised only in the realm of administration that lay beyond that encompassed by the Emperor's personal purview.

Alexander and his Young Friends thus combined the monocratic principle and the institutional precepts established by Paul I with their interpretation of Enlightenment thought to produce more rational allocations of administrative function which, although they vested ministers with greater monocratic authority, did not threaten the power and pre-eminence of the autocrat.[105] The nature and character of this achievement often have been obscured by undue emphasis on the "constitutionalism" of Alexander and his Young Friends and, especially, by historians' efforts to define that phenomenon in western liberal terms. Certainly Alexander and his associates used the term "constitution" in their writings and discussions about state affairs, but, as Marc Raeff has shown in his thoughtful and convincing analysis of the problem, the term held a very different meaning for them than it did for their western contemporaries. Alexander and his Young Friends therefore spoke and wrote in western terms, but, like Catherine II before them, they gave these terms meaning in the context of Russian, not European, experience. For them, the division of powers, a sacred element in the English and American constitutions, meant division of functions for the purpose of achieving an efficient state administration. The ideal to be achieved was a finely tuned machinery of administration that would govern the Russian Empire in an efficient and orderly fashion on the basis of precise regulations and laws.[106] To attain that goal, they agreed that the unlimited and undivided power of the autocrat must be preserved. In the established Russian political and administrative tradition, ministers, therefore, were to serve as the Emperor's personal agents, endowed with his personal commission *(poruchenie)* to assume specific responsibilities.

As they emerged in the early years of Alexander's reign, Russia's central administrative institutions thus were conceived to serve as extensions of the ruler's personal will. Stroganov insisted that it must be the Tsar's benevolent activity, "limited only by the principles of natural justice and universal morality" and extended throughout the state administration by his agents, Russia's ministers, that could ensure efficiency in directing the Empire's domestic affairs.[107] Yet the area of responsibility for which each minister was personally responsible was too broad to be controlled by his personal supervision. If the Emperor was to achieve his constitutional aim of creating a finely tuned administrative apparatus free from bureaucratic tyranny, it was necessary to establish procedures that would control the behavior of officials and guarantee that they functioned as he and his ministers wished. Ideally, this meant depersonalizing the Empire's central bureaucratic instruments to emphasize administration by institutions governed by regulations rather than by officials functioning under the Emperor's traditional personal commission. This effort was primarily the work of one of nineteenth-century Russia's greatest statesmen, M. M. Speranskii, who set out to redefine Russia's new ministerial system toward the end of Alexander's first decade on the throne.

Mikhail Mikhailovich Speranskii, son of a village priest, was born on January 1, 1772, and educated at the Aleksandro-Nevskii Seminary in St. Petersburg. He was appointed to the Seminary's faculty in 1792, but left it four years later to become the personal secretary of Prince A. B. Kurakin, the man whom Paul I appointed to the powerful position of *General-Prokuror* soon after his accession. As Kurakin's secretary, Speranskii gained administrative training at the highest levels of Russia's government, and he broadened his experience in the early nineteenth century as an assistant to D. P. Troshchinskii in the Senate, and then as a member of the staff of V. P. Kochubei, one of the Young Friends, who become Russia's first Minister of Internal Affairs. In mid-1803, Speranskii assisted Kochubei in drafting a full-scale

Nicholas I   *M. M. Speranskii*

structural organization of the new ministry along monocratic lines, and that served as the model for his proposals to reform the entire ministerial system less than a decade later.[108] Speranskii and Kochubei argued that a hierarchical organization of authority and responsibility was essential to the proper functioning of Russia's central administrative apparatus and regarded its absence as the most critical weakness in Russia's new central administration because it left the minister responsible for deciding even the most trivial questions. A rationally arranged chain of administrative authority throughout the ministry's structure, where each level in the hierarchy would have its own area of activity "to direct and be answerable for," could remedy that defect, they insisted, because lesser issues could be resolved in the course of their ascent upward through the administrative chain of command.[109]

Speranskii's opportunity to redefine the structure of Russia's central administration came after he became Alexander's leading adviser on questions of domestic reform and administration, and his General Statute on Ministries, published on June 23, 1811, served as the constitutional basis for Russia's central administration until January 1906. As such, it introduced into the Empire's ministerial system those hierarchical principles he considered so essential to the proper functioning of bureaucracy, but, although he sought to establish that division of function and delegation of authority characteristic of a modern bureaucratic structure, he subordinated Russia's new ministers to the autocrat so that they could function only as agents empowered to act by virtue of his personal commission. "Ministries represent the institutions by means of which the Supreme Executive Power acts upon all parts of the administration," the statute decreed. "All ministers are directly subordinate to the Supreme Power in all their activities," and "the essence of the power entrusted to ministers belongs exclusively to the executive catetory. Absolutely no law, statute, or any changes of those in existence," the new statute continued, "can be instituted by the authority of a minister. . . . The relationship of ministers to the Legislative Power consists in the fact that they can make recommendations about the need for a new law or statute or recommend changes in existing ones."[110]

This complete subordination of ministers to the autocrat, although fully in keeping with Russia's administrative and political tradition, carried within it the seeds of some of the most serious difficulties that the Empire's administration encountered during the next century. Most important, the principle of complete subordination to higher authority was extended further down in the bureaucracy, and during the reign of Nicholas I, this produced an exorbitant degree of formalism that seriously impeded effective administration, even though this sort of bureaucratic paralysis had not been Speranskii's intention. He had, in fact, championed a rational allocation of function and responsibility precisely to avoid such problems, but the basis for excessive formalism remained in his 1811 General Statute, not only because ministers were subjected to the authority of the autocrat but because Speranskii proposed no effective measures to overcome the tradition of complete subordination to higher authority within the ministries themselves. As the Statute specified, "the separation of various areas of administration within the ministries does not constitute the division of administration itself, for this, by its very nature, must always remain monocratic."[111] Within the context of Russian administrative tradition and practice, this meant that the authority of ministers over subordinate agencies became a reflection of that same power that the autocrat exercised over his ministers themselves, and, in the context of Russian administrative tradition, this power was by nature capricious and arbitrary. This became far more apparent during the Nicholaean era when, as a result of the Emperor's efforts to impose military characteristics upon his civil servants, the nature of such power became even more personalized. Speranskii's notion of administrative institutions governed by impersonal regulations thus rapidly gave way to administration predicated on caprice, and in further efforts to adjust Russia's instruments of authority to function more efficiently and effectively, Nicholas and his senior advisers personalized the nature of power even further. Continual surveillance was the means that Nicholas used to ascertain the state of his "command," and his ministers, many of them military men themselves, followed his example.

29

In contrast to Alexander's Young Friends, the minister-adjutants who served Nicholas I held a far more modest view of their role in policy-making and administration. Their perceptions of what their best efforts might reasonably achieve were more limited, and they saw themselves not as Stroganov's master physicians summoned to cure their nation's ills but as technicians called upon to adjust bureaucratic instruments that were fundamentally sound. Nevertheless, they expected to improve the ability of those instruments to respond to their nation's needs as they perceived them, and they set out to recruit better-educated and more talented young officials to staff their ministries. At the same time, they set out to refine the workings of their agencies with a confidence born of the belief that more precise regulation and supervision could make the bureaucracy as a whole operate more efficiently. "Each agency had to direct its attention to refining the manner in which it functioned," one eyewitness wrote. "Beginning in the 1830s, every department concentrated upon improvements . . . in the details of its internal administrative apparatus."[112]

Three of Nicholas's leading ministers were especially important in supporting that unique combination of talented officials dedicated to the ideal of effective administration from which Russia's enlightened bureaucracy emerged at mid-century. Minister of State Domains Count P. D. Kiselev, Minister of Internal Affairs Count L. A. Perovskii, and Minister of Justice Count V. N. Panin all served as living testimony to their Emperor's principles as they labored to reshape their agencies to reflect their shared creed of service, duty, and devotion to their Emperor. These men saw a beneficient paternalism in Minister of Public Instruction Uvarov's famous precepts of Orthodoxy, Autocracy, and Nationality, and they were convinced that, if properly applied, these would produce the best form of administration for the Empire. In sharp contrast to Russia's emerging radical intelligentsia, these statesmen confidently accepted the assumptions that underlay the Nicholas system and saw it as their main task to make their Emperor's vision of a service-state a reality. Although they all dedicated their lives to the Tsar's service, none remained constant to his principles for a longer time than did Pavel Dmitrievich Kiselev, whose career as a cavalry general, Imperial aide-de-camp, Minister of State Domains, and ambassador to France spanned more than a half-century. A dashing cavalry officer, Kiselev became an astute statesman and a courtly diplomat who possessed the rare ability to win the affection of men and command their best efforts on behalf of his Imperial masters.[113] "He is the favorite, most fashionable [salon] guest among all our great lords and, when he is in a good frame of mind, he is without doubt the most charming," remarked one courtier in the mid-1830s.[114]

As the eldest son of one of Moscow's most prominent noble families, Kiselev was groomed from early childhood for a career in Russia's service. Like most of his peers, he studied at home with a French tutor, and his mother, an Urusov princess, broadened his education by inviting some of Moscow's most talented writers and poets into her home. Among the intellectual and cultural elite who assembled at the Kiselev townhouse on Moscow's elegant Tverskaia were Karamzin and Ivan Dmitriev, as well as the young poets Aleksandr Turgenev and Prince P. A. Viazemskii, who became Kiselev's friends and shared with him their adolescent, sentimentalist dreams.[115] For most of them, such ideals made it possible as adults to accept the faults of the real world and divorce their feelings, thoughts, and inner spiritual lives from their duties as Russian officials. As we shall see further on, this became especially important in the experience of Count Panin, but, for Kiselev, sentimentalism was tempered by other influences which led him to view the process of change in more aggressive terms from the moment he chose to join the army rather than the foreign or civil service as had several of his closest friends.

Kiselev entered Russia's army as a cadet in January 1805 to serve on the staff of Quartermaster General Prince D. P. Volkonskii in St. Petersburg.[116] Soon he transferred to the Chevalier Guards and became part of an elite group of young noblemen who rose to high positions during the reign of Nicholas I. Most prominent were captain A. I. Chernyshev, later Minister of War (1827–1852), and staff captain V. V. Levashov, future president of the State Council's Department of State Economy (1839–1848) and president of the Committee of Ministers (1847–1848). They fought as comrades against Napoleon in 1807, and the shared dangers bound them for the rest of their lives. During the short years of peace that followed the Treaty of Tilsit, Prince A. S. Menshikov and A. F. Orlov joined their company. Together they prospered until they came to share places in the inner circles of the Tsar's advisers two decades later.[117] Kiselev thus quickly laid the foundations for a brilliant career; then, during Napoleon's invasion of 1812, he won the recognition that inspired Alexander I to name him an aide-de-camp and a general before he reached thirty.

Kiselev's first practical experience as a reformer came during the last decade of Alexander's reign when he transformed Russia's crumbling Second Army into a disciplined military force capable of defending the Empire's southern frontier, and this indicated the direction his views would take during the next quarter-century. Simplified administrative functions and centralized instruments of authority, he insisted, were the keys to his success.[118] At the same time, his readings of Chateaubriand, Benjamin Constant, Jeremy Bentham, and Adam Smith reinforced his caution in approaching social and economic renovation.[119] Beginning with a memorandum about serfdom in 1816, he urged Russia to begin a program of gradual social and economic change to prevent revolutionary upheavals from forcing such a course upon her.[120]

Although Kiselev's reform of the Second Army was a notable achievement for a young general, Nicholas imposed far more complex burdens upon him when he named him Plenipotentiary President of the Divans of Moldavia and Wallachia in the fall of 1829.[121] As Plenipotentiary President, Kiselev's task was the administrative, political, and economic renovation of a region plagued by corrupt police and oppressive lords whose serfs bore a yoke unequalled anywhere in Europe.[122] The difficulties proved too great and Kiselev's experience too limited, for he moved too quickly and on the basis of too little accurate information. In large measure, he failed, but his attempt convinced him that hard data and an expert understanding of the problems to be resolved were the most important prerequisites for effective administration and successful reform.[123] This conviction lay at the center of his views throughout his years as Russia's first Minister of State Domains. Again and again, he impressed this upon his subordinates, with important consequences for the future course of their efforts at social and economic renovation in Russia. From Kiselev's early insistence that policy decisions be based on accurate data evolved a broader movement in the Ministries of State Domains and Internal Affairs to expand the quantity of statistical information available to Russian statesmen.

Although Kiselev's efforts to lessen the burdens borne by the serfs in Wallachia and Moldavia were far from successful, they brought him to the Emperor's attention as a young statesman whose views on peasant reform might apply in Russia itself. "The thing most necessary of all for our Motherland," Kiselev insisted, "is the publication of an organic law which can equitably and precisely define the rights and obligations of serf-owning lords and tillers of the soil. All sensitive people recognize that it is necessary to provide institutions and guarantees for these millions of people before they get the idea of demanding them themselves."[124] Nicholas soon gave him an opportunity to test these precepts. "You will be my Chief of Staff for Peasant Affairs," he told him on February 17, 1836, when he named him head of the newly created Fifth Section of His Majesty's Own Chancery.[125]

The Emperor's decision to create the Fifth Section and to appoint Kiselev his Chief of Staff for Peasant Affairs stemmed from the failure of several secret committees to recommend ways for improving the conditions under which Russia's peasants lived.[126] Having failed to resolve this broader issue, Nicholas turned to improve the economic position of peasants living on state lands—the so-called *gosudarstvennye krest'iane*—in an effort to set an example that the nobility might be induced to follow.[127] As Chief of the Fifth Section and, after December 1837, as Minister of State Domains,[128] Kiselev tried to define the obligations between the *gosudarstvennye krest'iane* and the Imperial treasury in law rather than custom. At the same time, he set out to establish an efficient administration to deal with their affairs. Unlike his Imperial master, Kiselev shared Speranskii's opinion that rationally designed institutions held the key to effective administration, and he was certain that proper adjustments in bureaucratic instruments of authority would, by definition, better the economic position of Russia's state peasant communities.[129]

Kiselev insisted that change and reform could be initiated only at the center of the Imperial administration because "in Russia, nothing can be undertaken or completed without the leadership of the government."[130] Yet he was convinced that it was first necessary to assess economic and social conditions among the state peasants and judge the effectiveness of the state's administrative instruments if his ministry were to draft workable legislation. Therefore, he journeyed into the provinces to study these questions himself and, as a consequence of his on-the-scene investigations, urged a complete reversal in the state's attitude toward the peasant commune. Earlier in the century, Speranskii, Minister of Finance Kankrin, and several other prominent statesmen had urged the abolition of this fundamental unit of peasant society and administration in the Empire.[131] Kiselev now argued that the commune must be preserved as an instrument for strengthening state administration and control in the countryside if the government hoped to halt social and economic decay among its peasants.[132]

Initial investigations led Kiselev to a number of important conclusions but also convinced him that similar studies were needed for all provinces before an effective renovation of state peasant affairs could be undertaken. Between 1836 and 1840, he sent his "adjutants" (in this case agents of special commissions) into forty-seven Russian provinces, and, throughout his tenure, he commissioned further studies so that the central administration could respond more effectively to local conditions.[133] To undertake this task, and to establish the proper institutional base in St. Petersburg, he had to staff an entire new ministry with officials who were capable of initiative and the sort of independent judgment that usually was not found among Russian bureaucrats. Kiselev needed well-educated officials who had not yet become mired in the procedures and traditions of Russia's central administration, and he attempted to entice them from other agencies with promises of promotions, higher salaries, and opportunities to participate in policy-making decisions, even though such were, of necessity, limited to administrative issues. At the same time, he recruited new graduates from Russia's elite schools and universities.[134] He thus became the first of Nicholas's ministers to assemble those cadres whose ranks yielded up an enlightened bureaucracy at mid-century.

Kiselev's example soon was emulated by the man whom Nicholas appointed as Minister of Internal Affairs in September 1841. Lev Alekseevich Perovskii was born the son of Count A. K. Razumovskii's mistress on September 9, 1792. Like his half-brothers Nikolai and Vladimir, he was reared at the home of an aunt where he received a first-rate education from Razumovskii's chosen tutors, because the Count was determined to see his offspring well placed in Russia's service despite the circumstances of their birth.[135] Before his appointment as Russia's second Minister of Public Instruction in 1810, Count Razumovskii served as Rector of Moscow University, and it was while he held that post that Lev Alekseevich studied there. He too was touched by the sentimentalist currents so cherished by educated Moscow society, but, like Kiselev, he followed a military career while such Moscow friends as Dmitrii Bludov and S. S. Uvarov chose to serve in the elite Moscow Archive of the College of Foreign Affairs, where they could pursue their literary interests more readily. During Napoleon's invasion, Perovskii fought at Borodino, Malo-Iaroslavets, Lützen, and Leipzig. As a captain on the Guards General Staff in early 1815, he was wounded during the Hundred Days' campaign, recovered, and returned to Russia to become Chief Quartermaster of the Moscow Guards Division. He was one of the founders of the Union of Welfare in 1818, but resigned when its members chose revolution over reform in 1821.

Perovskii exchanged his military career for one in the Court and civil service when he exchanged his colonel's rank for that of a *statskii sovetnik* in the College of Foreign Affairs late in 1823. Some three years later, he transferred to the Department of Crown Lands of the Ministry of the Imperial Court, served as its vice-president until late 1840, as Deputy Minister of Crown Lands until 1852, and as Minister of Crown Lands until his death in 1856. During most of his tenure as Deputy Minister of Crown Lands, he also served as one of the most able Ministers of Internal Affairs to appear during the first half of the nineteenth century.[136]

The Department of Crown Lands administered the personal estates of the Imperial family, which held just under 600,000 male peasants at the time of Perovskii's transfer.[137] Because the income from these estates was designated for the private use of the Imperial family, their administration was a matter of direct personal concern to the Emperor, and that gave Perovskii an unparalleled opportunity to display his abilities as an administrator before Nicholas I himself. He launched a series

L. A. Perovskii   *P. D. Kiselev*

of reforms that more than doubled the direct income from Crown Lands in the quarter-century between 1820 and 1845 and, as a result, quickly established his reputation as a brilliant administrator.[138] His most important and innovative effort came in 1829, when he shifted the Department's basis of taxation from a levy on all male peasants (as had been applied to all privately owned serfs, state peasants, and Crown peasants since the reign of Peter the Great) to a system of rent dues based on the quality of the land they tilled. Perovskii's reform not only impressed Nicholas, but it became a model for the broadly reformed tax collection program that Kiselev and his subordinates implemented in the 1840s.[139]

Although a large responsibility (the Department of Crown Lands administered about five times as much land and peasants as did Russia's greatest serf-owners, the Sheremet'evs), Perovskii's department dealt with only about ten percent as much land and peasants as did Kiselev's new Ministry of State Domains in 1840.[140] Accustomed to smaller, more manageable administrative units, Perovskii suddenly confronted the vast operation of Russia's largest and most complex ministry when Nicholas appointed him Minister of Internal Affairs in 1841. From the first, he was appalled by the manner in which trivial duties sapped the energies of Russia's senior officials in capital and province alike. "The mechanical work of correspondence alone," he wrote in 1843, "surpasses the physical capabilities of the central offices of the provincial administration . . . and formalism devours the true essence of any administrative question." In his view, "all official correspondence ought to be merely the result of [a governor's] activity, not the main focus of it."[141] Yet he could do little to stem the tide. During his first year in office, the Ministry of Internal Affairs received and sent out a total of 22,326,842 separate documents; less than a decade later that figure had increased by more than forty percent, to 31,103,676.[142]

If he suffered defeat in his campaign against wasteful paperwork and useless formalities, Perovskii had more success in improving the manner in which his ministry functioned. First, he created a special chancellery to take on the flood of routine paperwork, and he soon extended that instrument to the offices of provincial governors and to all other central departments in his ministry. Assistant governors and deputy directors, he hoped, could free department directors and provincial governors from the pressures of routine administration so that they could become more directly involved in making policy. Together, he hoped that these officials could serve as a power base from which administrative reforms could be generated.[143]

Like the Emperor, Perovskii used his special chancellery as an extension of his administrative *persona* and therefore appointed to it men who held his closest confidence. Most important was the philologist V. I. Dal', his assistant in the Department of Crown Lands, whom he brought to the Ministry of Internal Affairs to head his special chancellery. Perovskii spoke of Dal' as his right hand and entrusted to him many tasks that Imperial ministers customarily reserved for their personal attention.[144] In doing so, he delegated responsibility more boldly than did most of his ministerial colleagues, and he extended the principles involved in that appointment much further downward in his ministry than they dared. Like Kiselev, he recruited well-educated young officials and drew them from a much wider variety of sources, including political exiles, recent graduates from elite schools and universities, university professors themselves, and men of established literary reputations.[145] Once they proved themselves, Perovskii gave these young men rare responsibilities for formulating policy and legislation, even though some of them were not yet out of their twenties. Under his tutelage, a number of prominent reformers of the 1860s gained their first practical experience with Russia's autocratic legislative process.

Like their Emperor, Kiselev and Perovskii continued to reserve all "command decisions" to themselves during the late 1830s and 1840s, but they used their ministries' departments to generate administrative policy in a manner unknown in Russia's bureaucracy at the time. In doing so, they established an institutional base that proved capable of broader effort at renovation some two decades later. Yet if the Russian bureaucracy was to find any significant success at the level of policy implementation, it needed far greater efficiency than it enjoyed during the first quarter of the nineteenth century. Count V. N. Panin, who became Russia's Minister of Justice in 1840, stressed "firm precision" in administration, even more than did Kiselev or Perovskii. He demanded subordination rather than encouraging independence, but his effort to make the Ministry of Justice function as a precise, efficient administrative instrument became an important factor in developing those administrative cadres from which Russia's enlightened bureaucracy emerged.[146]

Born in Moscow on March 28, 1801, Count Viktor Nikitich Panin came from a family whose stubborn arrogance had brought them disfavor, disgrace, and exile during the latter years of the eighteenth century, and he was acutely conscious that his ancestors' independent views had gotten them into trouble. As one scholar noted recently, Panin "went through life burdened by the sense that he had inherited a disgrace ordained for disobedience."[147] As a result, subordination to authority became the central element in his code of behavior. Panin obeyed his father, his teachers, and his superiors. Most of all, he obeyed his master, the Emperor. While the loyalty of Kiselev and Perovskii to their Emperor stemmed from their convictions as senior army officers, Panin's was born of the equally firm obedience of a Prussian Junker for, although Russian by birth, he became Prussian in manner and belief. "Because of my oath of allegiance," he once told Grand Duke Konstantin Nikolaevich, "I consider myself bound first of all to learn the views of my Emperor. If the Emperor has a view different from mine, then I consider it my duty to abandon my convictions immediately and even to act against them with the same, or even greater, energy than if I were acting according to my own opinions." Such subservience, combined with a love of order, precision, and regulation, recommended Panin highly to Nicholas I and to his son, who once remarked that Count Panin "has absolutely no convictions of his own, and his only concern is to please me."[148] Before his thirty-ninth birthday, Nicholas named this strange but intensely loyal man Russia's Minister of Justice.[149]

Panin's personality was as unpleasant as his career was brilliant. He was dry, cold, and unbending in his relations with equals. While Kiselev remained the dashing cavalryman, brilliant in high society, and Perovskii an elegant, well-educated lord, Panin was something of a recluse. His tall, ungainly frame misshapen by a pronounced stoop, he shunned polite society and conversation with others. It was reported that he kept parrots in his apartments and that he would converse with them because, when they replied, "they did not violate the rules of seniority."[150] It also was said that he had read Russia's entire *Digest of the Laws,* and that he had learned great chunks of it by heart. He obeyed his Emperor unquestioningly; he expected total subservience from his subordinates. Nikolai Semenov, who served under him for many years, remembered that "he considered the will of the sovereign to be sacred, and he thought the form of unlimited monarchical government to be the best of all possible systems. He fulfilled Imperial commands to the letter, without question, and demanded a similar obedience to his orders from his subordinates."[151] As Minister of Justice, Panin became "a real satrap, malevolent, fault-finding, merciless, and cold."[152]

If Panin seemed devoid of personal warmth, his devotion to duty, to the service, and to his Emperor had a positive effect upon the personnel of his ministry nonetheless. His belief in the law, as set forth in the *Digest of the Laws,* his adoration of firm precision, and his insistence that official matters be dealt with quickly and accurately were qualities rarely found in Russia's central administration. Even more than Kiselev and Perovskii, he insisted that the bureaucracy must function with the precision that he and his Imperial master so adored. As did the directors of the Ministries of State Domains and Internal Affairs, he required officials who were educated and diligent, for, as he once said, "an uneducated official, with only experience to his credit, [cannot] be truly useful."[153] Aside from the Imperial School of Jurisprudence, which graduated its first class of elite officials just as he became Minister, Panin recruited university graduates because he thought them "distinguished in service affairs by their well-founded knowledge," and he brought a significant number of them into his ministry.[154] As one of his subordinates later recalled, many of these men eventually found the rigid formalism of his regime "difficult and even intolerable for a person wishing to be independent to some degree," and a number fled to other agencies during the 1850s and early 1860s.[155] But this flight did not occur before some of Panin's recruits had formed a cadre that created the institutional base for reform work within the Ministry of Justice. S. I. Zarudnyi's so-called "school" in the Ministry's Consultation and the Moscow Departments of the Senate were especially important in that regard.[156] There, such eminent figures as Zarudnyi, K. P. Pobedonostsev, and D. A. Rovinskii, who played a major role in drafting the Judicial Reform Statutes of 1864, assembled during the last decade of Nicholas I's reign. Although they rejected Panin's rigidity and formalism, these younger men preserved his emphasis on precision, accountability, and loyalty to the Emperor. Under his tutelage, they developed an expertise in the law and an awareness of its shortcomings that was unequalled in Russia's administration.

Men such as Kiselev, Perovskii, and Panin belonged to the first generation of statesmen who began their careers in Russia's ministerial administration. Unlike such great Catherinian lords as Gavrila Derzhavin and Dmitrii Troshchinskii, they had not participated in its creation in the provinces, nor had they, like Alexander I's Young Friends and Speranskii, played a role in its establishment in St. Petersburg. Beginning their careers just as Russia's ministerial administration developed its institutional base, they were acutely aware of those limitations and shortcomings that emerged during its first years of testing. Because they considered the instruments of Russia's ministerial administration imperfect, Perovskii and Kiselev adjusted those agencies that lay within their ministries to improve their overall functioning; by contrast, Panin adjusted only the procedures by which various departments within the Ministry of Justice functioned.

Although Kiselev and Perovskii differed from Panin about the nature and scope of adjustments required to make Russia's ministerial administration function properly, they were more closely in agreement about the sort of personnel they required. As the sons and grandsons of men who had served the autocrat personally in the highest levels of government, they had been raised on the Karamzinian maxim that "a wise government finds the means to encourage the good tendencies in public officials and to restrain the inclination toward evil," and that "the minister [should] answer ... for the choice of leading officials."[157] Equally important, they understood that the more complex problems that Russia's ministerial administration faced required officials who were better educated. Finally, they knew that bribery, corruption, and incompetence among lower-ranking officials must be eliminated if Russia's ministerial administration were to function properly.[158]

Certain that better-educated, better-trained, and more honest officials would produce better administration, Kiselev, Perovskii, and Panin recruited them from among the graduates of Russia's elite schools and universities. Yet the young men they brought into their ministries came from different backgrounds, shared different experiences, and held different views about administration and change than they. While their mentors in the service remained convinced that the precepts of the Nicholas system, when properly applied, would produce the best form of administration for Russia, such young officials as Andrei Zablotskii-Desiatovskii, Nikolai Miliutin, Sergei Zarudnyi, and a number of their friends and close associates, came to understand that broader changes were needed. Procedural and institutional adjustments, they realized, could not resolve the problems that faced Russia and the Imperial administration. Some effective means had to be found to change policy and, once changed, to implement it effectively. Neither could be achieved under the regimes of such statesmen as Perovskii, Kiselev, or Panin, whose efforts to make their ministries more "efficient" produced the "heyday of formalism." Mere adjustment in the bureaucratic instruments of authority was not enough to embark upon the program of conservative renovation that Russia required, but the next step was by no means clear.[159] A search for the means to go beyond the limitations posed by these elder statesmen's views occupied progressive young Russian officials throughout the 1840s and well into the 1850s.

ChAPTER 2

New Men and New Aspirations

*"Their ideal was the introduction of justice
into all spheres of life. . . . Along the way to
attaining this ideal they had two guideposts:
hard work and a sense of duty."*
A. P. Zablotskii-Desiatovskii

The young officials whom Kiselev, Perovskii, and Panin recruited into the lower echelons of their ministries came from impoverished noble families with traditions of service to Russia. Their fathers, who frequently had started their careers in the lower ranks, had reached the middle levels of Russia's army or bureaucracy; and, from the moment the sons grew beyond infancy, they were encouraged to follow in their fathers' footsteps. At considerable expense and personal sacrifice, these men employed tutors to give their sons an elementary education. As soon as they were old enough, they were enrolled in elite schools where the ideals of service to the state formed an integral part of their adolescent experience. At such institutions as the Lyceum at Tsarskoe Selo, the Boarding Schools for Sons of the Nobility at Moscow and St. Petersburg Universities, and then at the universities themselves, they were conditioned to think of themselves as part of an elite, especially because they were distinguished by impressive educations in a milieu where such were uncommon.[1] These young men graduated from school intent upon serving Tsar and country and anxious to build successful careers for themselves in the process.

Young men who nourished ambitions to better their social and economic status through successful careers in the civil service automatically turned their steps toward St. Petersburg, only to encounter those many frustrations that lay in wait for all but those with close ties to the

Imperial Court. Victims of a painful metamorphosis, these young men were transformed from members of an elite into the rank and file of a shabby clerical army to which the most inconsequential and demeaning tasks were assigned. Like Aleksandr Aduev, Goncharov's university graduate who entered the bureaucracy expecting to deal with important affairs of state but found himself assigned to menial clerical duties instead, these young men at first felt trapped by a system that gave little immediate recognition to their talent and education. Regarded as nameless cogs in the endlessly interlocking wheels of the machinery of Russian officialdom, they earned salaries that barely enabled them to subsist in the midst of St. Petersburg's luxury and opulence.[2]

These years of material deprivation and psychological degradation were critical to the making of successful careers, for it was at this time that young men had to find a means to rise above that faceless mass of petty officials among whom they had been cast. They had to succeed or be condemned to lives of drudgery, misery and, in their own terms, failure. Aside from family connections, which most did not have, one of the most effective ways to gain attention in the bureaucracy was to become an expert in some field. In the Ministries of Internal Affairs and State Domains especially, Perovskii and Kiselev sought out men from all over Russia who could provide those accurate data about local conditions which they thought essential to the role they envisioned for their ministries, and a young official who could assemble such information, sift it efficiently, and present it in the form of a comprehensive and comprehensible report, stood a good chance to begin a successful career under their tutelage.

The process of becoming such a specialist involved more than theoretical study, however. The information recorded in provincial offices usually was grossly inadequate for even the most crude statistical work, and suspicious local officials often were uncooperative. Therefore, it was necessary for an ambitious young man to visit the area in question in order to compile the necessary statistical information from personal study and observation, and this often unpalatable task posed one of the major dilemmas in the lives of young bureaucrats who aspired to higher positions.[3] On the one hand, chances for visibility and promotion were greater in the capital; on the other, to obtain the expert status that could be an important factor in gaining the attention of his superiors, an official might have to spend months or even years in the provinces. An ambitious young official thus had to spend sufficient time in the provinces to gain the expertise needed to win attention yet not spend so much time away from the capital that his superiors lost sight of him.[4] The effort to strike a balance between service in the St. Petersburg bureaucracy and visits to the provinces was characteristic of nearly all the men whom we shall discuss in this chapter. All received assignments as agents of special commissions in the provinces during the first decade of their careers, and some spent nearly all of the 1840s away from St. Petersburg. Not all properly balanced service in the provinces against service in the capital, with the result that they sometimes rose to responsible positions within their respective ministries but never achieved influence as policy-makers. When it came time to draft the Great Reforms, these men did not play a visible, public part.[5]

Elite education, good fortune, devotion to ministerial affairs, and a willingness to forsake temporarily the comparative comforts of the capital for a more difficult life in the provinces served to advance the fortunes of a number of young officials who rose to responsible positions under Kiselev, Perovskii, and Panin in a manner that generally was uncharacteristic of the careers of most civil servants. They rose quickly, often earning the rank of *statskii sovetnik* in twelve to fifteen years, so that they reached senior rank before they became so steeped in the bureaucracy's formalistic tradition that they could not envision different approaches to the more complex problems Russia faced at mid-century. For these men, the period between the late 1830s and early 1840s was a time of study and personal development. They examined Russian conditions, re-cast their views about the types of reforms needed to improve the quality of life in the Empire, and developed a new vision of the bureaucratic instruments Russia required. They soon became a living body of collective knowledge about Russian provincial life that was unequalled in the Imperial administration.

Andrei Zablotskii-Desiatovskii and Russia's State Peasants

Perhaps no issue of the 1840s commanded the attention of educated Russians more urgently than did serfdom. Few senior officials or great serf-owners believed that it could continue for long without major transformations. "The question of the abolition of serfdom astonishes no one now," wrote one official in 1841,[6] and, just a few years later, Perovskii told Nicholas that "time and new [economic] relationships have completely altered the view of the educated *pomeshchiki* toward serfdom. . . . The *pomeshchiki* are themselves beginning to understand that the serfs are a burden to them and that it would be desirable to alter these mutually disadvantageous relationships."[7] Statesmen, bureaucrats, and the educated public therefore had to ask how the dilemmas posed by serfdom might be resolved, in what manner the relationship between master and serf ought to be changed and, the most fearsome question of all: when should substantive alterations in the serf order be undertaken? These were cursed questions indeed, and they plagued Russians throughout the Nicholaean era.

Because the economic well-being of the Empire's privileged elite class—the nobility—was involved in any effort to alter serfdom, it became more difficult to agree on the means for resolving these questions. For Russian noblemen who had suffered the elemental force of peasant wrath from time to time and for state authorities who valued the preservation of order above all else, the fear that an emancipation might usher in an era of peasant violence posed very real dilemmas. "The educated *pomeshchiki*," Perovskii warned Nicholas, "fear the consequences of freedom [for the serfs], knowing the unbridled nature of the masses."[8] Throughout the second quarter of the century, statesmen made little progress toward resolving these dilemmas but continued to hope that the passage of time somehow would render them less complex. "Questions which now seem vexing will doubtless be untangled through experience,"[9] Nicholas once remarked. He evidently hoped that Kiselev's work with the state peasants could become one of the major sources of such experience. By concentrating on them, he thought that the government might set an example that perhaps could induce the nobility to limit serfdom on their estates.[10]

Few officials became so deeply involved in the study of life among the state peasants during the 1840s as did Andrei Parfenovich Zablotskii-Desiatovskii, chief of the Statistical Section of the Department of Rural Economy in Kislev's Ministry of State Domains. Born in Chernigov province, Zablotskii was a member of an impoverished, but ancient, noble family. He grew up in the Ukrainian countryside, where his father managed the estates of a rich lord, studied at the local *gimnaziia* at Novgorod-Seversk, and lived in close daily contact with serfs throughout his childhood. We know little else about Zablotskii's early life, nor do we know the impressions that his broad experience with serf life made upon him. As a well-educated, but serf-less, landowner, his father must have realized that education was the only key that might unlock for his son the door to success in the state service, and, almost certainly, he encouraged him to study at the University of Moscow, where Zablotskii graduated with a gold medal in 1827, and received an advanced degree in 1832.[11]

The primitive state of statistical studies in Russia's central administration was a problem Zablotskii encountered almost from the moment he entered the Ministry of Internal Affairs in 1832. Western European states long since had incorporated statistical agencies into their bureaucratic structures, but the first in Russia was established in the Ministry of Internal Affairs at Speranskii's urging only in 1802. Transferred to the short-lived Ministry of Police a decade later, this organization did little more than compile the crude data that provincial governors submitted about population movements. At about the same time, the Ministry of Finance began to collect information about state peasants, the output of state mines, foreign and domestic trade, and tax collections. But it had no separate agency for this purpose and did not compile its data on a regular or comprehensive basis.[12] It was not until 1835 that the Ministry of Internal Affairs, the central agency in the Empire most broadly concerned with domestic policy, incorporated a regular statistical office into its structure. Konstantin Arsen'ev, tutor to Grand Duke Aleksandr Nikolaevich in history and statistics, became its first director. Despite Zablotskii's very junior status, Arsen'ev chose him as secretary of this new agency and supported his promotion to the rank of *kollezhskii asessor* at the age of twenty-seven.[13]

Under Arsen'ev's tutelage Zablotskii's early career bore every mark of success, but he transferred to Kiselev's Fifth Section in early 1837 nonetheless. We do not know for certain why he chose to stake his future on the chance of advancement in a new and untried state agency, but a number of factors may have influenced his decision. Most obviously, the newly organized Fifth Section offered broader opportunities for promotion and was less controlled by those formal routines and procedures that he and men like him so despised.[14] The Fifth Section offered him a chance to organize a small agency according to his own precepts, and that attraction may have been heightened by Kiselev himself, who had already recruited V. I. Karneev, Director of the Ministry of Internal Affairs' Economic Department. Karneev may in turn have urged Zablotskii, as a young official of recognized promise in his agency, to follow him.[15]

Zablotskii's transfer to the Fifth Section placed him on one of the most unusual bureaucratic staffs in Russia, its talent equalled perhaps only by the group of unusually well-educated young officials Speranskii had assembled in the Second Section during the 1820s to codify Russia's laws.[16] The majority of Speranskii's jurists came from wealthy aristocratic backgrounds and therefore shared what one scholar has called a "new nonchalance, a sophisticated and detached acceptance of the frailties of the system."[17] Most of them never experienced the vicissitudes of life in the lower depths of the bureaucracy and, because of their high birth, remained relatively isolated from the reality of Russian provincial life. Such men never could share Zablotskii's deep concern about the gap between senior state officials and the problems for which they were responsible, while he never could share their blasé self-confidence that even without careful study, a statesman's superior intellect could transcend that administrative abyss and formulate workable solutions to economic and administrative crises. "Governmental activity," Zablot-skii insisted, "ought to be based not upon theoretical understanding, but on the study of subjects in real life."[18] No longer should the Russian Empire be governed "simply upon the basis of practical knowledge about administrative affairs [*deloproizvodstvo*], with no specialized study of the problems that were dealt with."[19]

In Kiselev's new Ministry of Internal Affairs, Karneev's Third Department was the first agency in St. Petersburg to recruit men almost solely on the basis of educational qualifications. The result was impressive. Like Zablotskii, a future member of the Editing Commissions of 1859–1860, Ivan Arapetov, had just graduated from Moscow University when he entered the Third Department as a translator.[20] A. K. Girs, who played a major role in the urban studies that Nikolai Miliutin's Municipal Section produced between 1842 and 1856, had graduated from the Lyceum at Tsarskoe Selo with a silver medal only three years before, was dissatisfied with his position in the Ministry of Justice, and entered the Third Department as a deputy chief of an office section.[21] K. K. Grot, like Girs a recent graduate from the Lyceum, also transferred to the Ministry of State Domains in 1838 for much the same reasons. Grot later became Governor of Samara province.[22] V. A. Insarskii, later a close associate of Prince A. I. Bariatinskii in the Caucasus, became chief of an office section under Karneev,[23] as did A. F. Shtakel'berg, a St. Petersburg University graduate who later studied urban economy and administration in the Baltic provinces.[24] Konstantin Veselovskii, a member of the Imperial Russian Academy of Sciences at the age of thirty-seven and one of Russia's most noted statisticians, also found his first service post in Zablotskii's statistical bureau in the Third Department, and he summoned younger graduates from his *alma mater* at Tsarskoe Selo to join him there.[25] As a result, an agency that had been unusual for the high level of its officials' education from the beginning became even more so.

Most of these young men shared a common aristocratic background, although few were rich. For them, state service offered the best means to win status, privilege, and power and to rise above their middling noble origins. To the degree that such is possible in a bureaucracy, they possessed a rare measure of self-confidence and that led them to forsake the security of time-in-grade promotions in other state agencies for the prospect of more rapid promotions based on merit. They were thus distinguished from most bureaucrats by their willingness to let ability, rather than longevity, determine the course of their careers. They were so confident of their ability that, a few years later, they transferred *en masse* into Miliutin's new Municipal Section, at the cost of their seniority, to take advantage of the opportunities it offered to develop new specialties in assembling and analyzing urban statistics.

Zablotskii and his colleagues thought that decisions should be made not according to "general rules of bureaucracy, but on the bases of knowledge and enlightenment."[26] Zablotskii himself characterized this new attitude even more forcefully. In describing his colleagues, he once wrote:

> Their ideal was the introduction of justice into all spheres of life. . . . No one preached about this ideal. As naturalists say, it was conceived among them spontaneously. Along the path to attaining this ideal, they had two guide-posts: hard work and a sense of duty. In hard work, they saw not only the means without which it is impossible to improve one's position in society legitimately, but also a necessary requirement for the full enjoyment of life. In the fulfillment of their duty, they saw a basic law of morality.[27]

The men who entered the Third Department of the Ministry of State Domains in the mid- to late 1830s thus were officials of a new breed: talented, well-educated, willing to let ability stand as a measure of their worth and, because of their relatively impoverished backgrounds, anxious to make their mark in the state service. Under Zablotskii's leadership they found an opportunity to test their talents during the late 1830s and 1840s.

Zablotskii and his associates first had to examine earlier proposals for improving the administration of the state peasants' domains and then codify the legislative materials that related to them. Then, as a preliminary step to preparing new plans for administrative reform, they compiled the scattered data available about state peasants. To an important extent basing their actions upon Speranskii's example, they expressed a deep faith in the value of such preparatory work. In an administration where few statesmen ever overcame bureaucratic inertia sufficiently to produce large-scale administrative reforms, the success of Speranskii's efforts loomed large. Speranskii first had reorganized the administration of Russia's vast Siberian domains and had followed that achievement by completing within a decade that task of codification that had defied the best efforts of Russian administrators and jurists since Peter the Great. During the 1830s (Zablotskii wrote some years later), "the works of a statesman who combined a rare mind with practical ability—Count Speranskii—began to influence our administration."[28] Speranskii's achievement and personal example thus had a great impact on the administrative reform processes of the 1830s. "In addition to being of immediate use in daily administration, the *Digest of the Laws* had other very important influences," Zablotskii remembered. "Setting forth in their totality the existing laws on each area of administration, the *Digest* revealed . . . all their shortcomings, their insufficiencies, and contradictions, which, until that time, had gone unnoticed."[29] Speranskii's successful compilation of the laws thus instilled in Zablotskii and his friends a deep faith in the virtue of codifying materials before undertaking any administrative venture. Speranskii's application of codification techniques to Russia's laws soon raised the process itself to a level of truth in which Imperial statesmen believed until the twentieth century.

Because Zablotskii played no role in the actual preparation of the eight laws that the Ministry of State Domains drafted under Kiselev's guidance between 1837 and 1840 to improve the state's administration of its peasants, their substance need not concern us here.[30] Those laws dealt exclusively with administrative issues because Kiselev saw effective administration as the key to improving life among the state peasants. "The main thing [is to work out] effective administrative measures," he once wrote.[31] More important for our purposes here, Kiselev ordered detailed investigations of the manner in which the state peasants lived, and Zablotskii played an important part in these throughout the late 1830s and 1840s. His first official assignment to study local peasant life came in early 1837, even before his formal appointment to the Fifth Section. Under the direction of the famous academician Petr Keppen, a statistician even more renowned than Arsen'ev during the 1830s, Zablotskii and Nikolai Miliutin, a young official from the Economic Department in the Ministry of Internal Affairs, studied life in Southern Russia's state peasant villages during the spring and summer.[32] Both Zablotskii and Miliutin received valuable statistical training from Keppen, and they began a friendship that lasted throughout their lives.

The pattern of Zablotskii's and Miliutin's assignments diverged sharply during the decade after they served with Keppen in Southern Russia. Miliutin soon became deeply involved in the legislative process itself, and his work confined him to St. Petersburg's chanceries, while Zablotskii continued to learn more about rural life as he pursued official assignments from the Baltic to the Caucasus. Zablotskii's isolation from the legislative process endowed him with an unusually broad view of Russian peasant life, from which he concluded that the problems he witnessed in Russia's countryside stemmed from the institution of serfdom. Zablotskii expressed a deep sense of moral outrage at the injustice of the serf system, for he believed in the law and saw in its statutes the way to progress. "The first condition by which . . . the success of all administration is guaranteed is the understanding of lawfulness," he once remarked.[33] Yet he found little that resembled legality or lawfulness in the relationships between master and serf. "Not being able to possess property, the serf cannot defend his rights in the courts," he pointed out in 1841. "What a strange state of affairs," he concluded. "Half of the state's inhabitants, according to the law, are excluded from any protection of the law."[34]

If serfdom contradicted Zablotskii's ideal of a society based on law, he also indicted the system on economic and moral grounds. Because it offered no incentive for the serf to produce anything beyond the bare minimum, Russia's agricultural and industrial output could not be expanded through increased productivity.[35] This did not mean that individual serf-owners could not increase their incomes, Zablotskii argued, but that could only be accomplished if the *pomeshchiki* took more and left their peasants with less.[36] Thus, serfdom was one man's direct exploitation of many in a relationship ruled by the highest degree of caprice. There were few legal restraints upon a nobleman's dealings with his peasants, and, in Zablotskii's opinion, that had led to a profound erosion of peasant morality. "The poverty of the majority of the nobles' peasants and the frequent changes in their fortunes," he wrote in a memorandum to Kiselev, "have given birth to an important vice among them—the loss of shame." In turn, this led peasants to prefer begging to honest work.[37] The hopelessness of such a life, Zablotskii reported, turned peasants into drunkards, and *pomeshchiki* even encouraged that vice by producing spirits on their estates and selling them to their serfs.[38]

From his observations about peasant life in the late 1830s and early 1840s, Zablotskii concluded that Kiselev's efforts to refine the state's instruments of administration and authority could not improve Russia's rural economy. In his view, none of the major impediments to bringing greater prosperity to Russia's state peasants could be resolved by administrative *fiat*. The first of these obstacles stemmed from the quality of the statistical data that central government offices received from provincial officials. "Whoever has looked over any of the materials compiled by lower-level administrative agencies," Zablotskii complained, "knows how tangled and inaccurate they are. The consequences of this are evident in those legislative proposals which are based upon such incomplete data."[39] The only solution was to send into the provinces trusted officials who were capable of obtaining the sorts of data which central agencies required. First as chief of the Statistical Section of the Third Department, then as a member of his ministry's scientific council, and, finally, as head of the Third Department itself (by then re-named the Department of Rural Economy), Zablotskii developed a body of accurate information about state peasant life in the Ministry of State Domains so that legislative proposals could take conditions in the countryside more accurately into account.

Zablotskii's efforts to assemble accurate information about provincial life aided his attempts to break down the peasants' ignorance about modern agriculture which, in his view, was the second major obstacle to increasing rural prosperity in Russia. During the early 1840s, he enlisted the help of Prince V. F. Odoevskii, a colleague in the Ministry of State Domains and a close personal friend, to publish a series of booklets which bore the title *Sel'skoe chtenie.* The impetus for the project grew out of the Third Department's efforts to prepare a "catechism on the most important principles for successful agriculture" that would instruct state peasants about how to farm more effectively.[40] Though admirable in conception, the task fell upon a number of overworked officials who kept setting it aside as more pressing (though usually less important) administrative matters demanded their attention. Convinced by late 1842 that the catechism would be a long time in coming (in fact, it still was in preparation at the end of Nicholas's reign), Zablotskii decided to pursue another course.[41] His official inquires about conditions in state peasant villages, as well as the secret studies about serf life that Kiselev had commissioned him to undertake, convinced him that the spiritual and moral degeneration of Russia's rural population had become so serious that direct action could not wait.

Four *Sel'skoe chtenie* booklets appeared between 1843 and 1848, as Zablotskii and Odoevskii enlisted the services of such writers as Vladimir Dal' and Count V. A. Sollogub. Their writings combined a variety of moral aphorisms with injunctions about the virtue of sobriety and simply stated agricultural advice to peasant readers. "If you want a good harvest, choose the type of soil best suited to the seed you intend to plant," they explained. "Choose the very best seed. If you sow poor seed, you might as well sow sand. Your labor and time will be wasted." Such advice was combined with folksy tales about "How the Peasant Spiridon Taught the Peasant Ivan Not to Drink Vodka and What Happened as a Result" and "An Accounting of How Much Money Can Be Saved by Not Drinking Vodka," as Zablotskii set out to curb peasant alcoholism.[42] The impact of his efforts is impossible to measure, of course. But it is certain that Zablotskii found an audience for his preachings. Each of the *Sel'skoe chtenie* booklets went through several printings totaling well over 30,000 copies before 1848, at which time Russia's senior statesmen, with the example of the Galician peasant revolts of 1846 still fresh in their minds, grew fearful for the security of the Empire's rural areas and stopped him from publishing further issues.[43]

By the mid-1840s, Zablotskii had concluded that administrative regulations could not restructure social and economic relationships in Russia and that the state must in fact alter the attitudes of Russia's rural dwellers if it wished to improve the quality of provincial life. During the late 1840s and early 1850s, Zablotskii expanded his ministry's efforts to establish agricultural schools and model farms, but he did not abandon his efforts to influence serf life more directly. For the moment, he altered his focus and turned to the serf-owners themselves in order to acquaint them with technological and agronomical innovations. For that purpose, he sponsored regional agricultural exhibitions and encouraged the development of new agricultural societies. For the mass of petty serf-owners—that 80 percent of the nobility who owned a mere 20 percent of the serfs—his efforts at enlightenment evolved directly from *Sel'skoe chtenie*. Therefore, in the late 1840s, Zablotskii published a series of "Agricultural Aphorisms" in the progressive journal *Otechestvennye zapiski*, which presented Russia's squires with agricultural principles only slightly more sophisticated than those he had prepared for their peasants a few years earlier.[44]

Although Zablotskii continued to learn about rural life and the problems that Russia's peasant millions faced during the 1840s, the nature of his administrative duties continued to shield him from the complex autocratic legislative process upon which the success of any gradual transformation of rural Russia depended. That task became a central focus of the efforts of his close friend Nikolai Miliutin, who became deeply involved in legislative work in St. Petersburg while Zablotskii studied Russia's countryside.

Nikolai Miliutin and the Autocratic Legislative Process

At the beginning of the nineteenth century, Alexander I, his Young Friends, and Speranskii had tried with limited success to create a state administration in which the precepts of autocracy were combined with the rule of law. They hoped to achieve their goal through the instruments of Russia's new ministerial government, which delegated executive authority to the Empire's ministers but left legislative power exclusively in the hands of the autocrat. Yet, if Russia's laws denied legislative power to her chief ministers, they did not exclude them from the legislative process, for their ministers were empowered to make "recommendations about the need for a new law, or statute, or recommend changes in existing ones."[45] During the Nicholaean era, Imperial ministers used their authority to recommend increasingly complex legislation, and this had the practical consequence of bestowing considerable legislative power upon them. Well before the middle of the century, ministerial legislative "recommendations" evolved into lengthy and precisely worded documents drafted according to the format of statutes issued by the Ruling Senate. As a result, the autocratic legislative process was expanded to include a series of negotiations among the Emperor, the State Council, and Russia's ministers and their subordinate executive organs.

One of the most complex areas of bureaucratic activity in which a young official could gain expert status during the 1830s and 1840s was the functioning of this legislative process. To do so was especially difficult, not only because opportunities to engage in planning reform were very limited but because it was rare indeed for a young official even to encounter the devious processes that senior officials employed to resist or permit change. Nikolai Miliutin, who entered the Ministry of Internal Affairs in November 1835, thus remains an unusual example of an ambitious young official who used to good advantage a rare opportunity to guide reform legislation through Russia's central bureaucracy. Miliutin's unique experience in the 1840s became especially valuable to him and a number of his colleagues when they began to draft Russia's Great Reform legislation after the Crimean War.

Nikolai Alekseevich Miliutin's family had risen to prominence in the 1750s and was numbered among Moscow's richest nobles when Alexander I ascended the throne in 1801.[46] Extravagance and mismanagement dissipated the family fortune quickly, and when Miliutin was born on June 6, 1818, their standard of living had diminished to a mere shadow of its former brilliance. Because his parents no longer could afford to live in Moscow, Miliutin spent the first decade of his life at Titovo amidst the decaying elegance of what only a half-century before had been a flourishing noble demense in Kaluga province with more than 1,000 serfs and seventy mills producing velvets and damasks.[47]

Although nature had endowed Miliutin's father with few entrepreneurial skills, he was well educated by early nineteenth-century standards and knew that his sons' best chance for success in life lay in the state service. Thanks to the influence of Kiselev, his wife's eldest brother, he enrolled his three eldest sons in the Boarding School for Sons of the Nobility at Moscow University, where much of the teaching was done by prominent scholars from the university's own faculty.[48] Touched by that romanticism that consumed sensitive Russian noble youths in the 1820s and early 1830s, Miliutin remained a supreme dilettante during his six years at the Boarding School. Often plagued by "melancholic and agitated states of mind," he extolled the virtues of sensitivity and lived out a variety of adolescent fantasies about careers for which he was unprepared and unsuited.[49]

Miliutin's fantasy world was partly an effort to escape a painful awareness that he, his brothers, and his parents all were abjectly dependent on the Kiselevs.[50] He found such dependence a bitter pill, and one might speculate that it colored many of his attitudes during his adolescent years. Once in Russia's civil service, he clearly displayed a brilliant mind and a rare ability to grasp the essence of complex affairs of state. Yet during those years when each day in the classroom reminded him of his dependence on Kiselev's patronage, Miliutin exhibited scarcely a glimmer of these talents. Kiselev had opposed his sister's marriage to Miliutin's father, whom he considered too close to middle age, too inept, and too far beneath her social status, and Kiselev never forgave him for taking his cherished sister away from the luxurious family nest to the spartan surroundings of the Miliutin provincial estate.[51] The "charity" he doled out never could be mistaken for kindness or generosity. Miliutin knew whence came his chance for the elite education that offered him a chance at a successful career, and his reaction appears to have been stubborn, almost self-destructive, rejection. Tensions between uncle and nephew continued for several decades, until Miliutin could approach Kiselev on a more equal footing. Not until the early 1860s did nephew and uncle begin to enjoy a warm relationship.[52]

Among other things, Miliutin's adolescent fantasies centered upon a life devoted to literature. His efforts to realize that dream revealed his meager literary talent, for his endeavors went no further than shallow imitations of Byron and Aleksandr Bestuzhev-Marlinskii.[53] Miliutin's emotional commitment to romanticism in the 1830s differed sharply from the more deeply rooted variety that was central to the intellectual experiences of the fervent Moscow youths of his generation. For such young men as Nikolai Ogarev, Aleksandr Herzen, Nikolai Stankevich —even the supreme realist Vissarion Belinskii—romanticism exalted their spirits and gave them that sense of common purpose which enabled them to stand together even against the authority of the autocrat. Briefly, Miliutin, too, was critical of the existing order, but in a more shallow and self-interested vein. To be sure, he found life in the lower ranks of St. Petersburg's clerical army dreary, and he proclaimed bitterly to all who would listen that chancery work was an *"existence manquée,"*[54] a bottomless sea of bureaucratic mud that sucked at his well-worn boots and threatened to draw him into its lower depths. But, in sharp contrast to Russia's alienated intelligentsia of the 1830s, Miliutin soon carved out an emotionally satisfying life within the confines of that very bureaucracy they so despised. In patronage-conscious St. Petersburg, where, as one observer noted, success usually came through deceit and "by the fortunate chance of drawing attention to oneself by a clever trick or by successful flattery,"[55] he found that recognition he had craved ever since he first entered the Boarding School.

Such did not come immediately, but at least a small recognition of his ability came in 1837, when a group of talented young officials and scholars invited him to compile data about trade, guilds, and small industries in Russia's cities and ports for *A Library of Commercial Knowledge.* Most prominent among the contributors were Zablotskii, his mentor Arsen'ev, and the statistician G. P. Nebolsin, who thought that before Russia could embark upon the path to progress, her officials must assemble accurate information about the economic and social conditions within her borders. More important, perhaps, this undertaking assured Miliutin that worthwhile tasks could be found in Russia's bureaucratic world and thus introduced him to that study of urban problems which consumed much of his attention for the next two decades.[56] Within the inner reaches of the Ministry of Internal Affairs' Economic Department, he no longer was dependent on Kiselev's charity, and he began to gain that measure of self-esteem needed for success.

Miliutin's work on *A Library of Commercial Knowledge* did not immediately free him from the lower depths of St. Petersburg's clerical world. Most probably because he had been so dependent on Kiselev's charity during his adolescent years, he found repugnant that sort of patronage needed to advance a career in Russia's capital. Eventually, powerful men aided his career, but he remained unable to bring himself to curry their favor.[57] Rejecting flattery as a means of making his way, he set out to command his superiors' attention as an efficient civil servant. That at first proved difficult because the Minister of Internal Affairs at the time was Count D. N. Bludov, an official whom one courtier characterized as a nonentity in the ranks of Russia's statesmen.[58] Such a remark may have been more uncharitable than was warranted, but it was true that Bludov suffered from an uncritical faith in the merits of Russia's ministerial administration, and he tolerated ineptness, even incompetence, among his subordinates.[59] Courtly, urbane, extremely well-educated, and possessor of considerable literary talent, he was not a man to urge a better understanding of conditions in an Empire he thought already well governed. Bludov was not the kind of statesman upon whom a young man of Miliutin's type would make an impression, and Miliutin found few opportunities for advancement under Bludov's stewardship. The years from 1835 to 1839 became for Miliutin a time of preparation and training in the language and practice of bureaucracy which Bludov himself once described as "habit, love of precision, and subordination."[60]

A change of ministers in 1839 provided Miliutin with new opportunities for advancement. Count A. G. Stroganov, and the energetic and forceful Perovskii who followed him as Minister of Internal Affairs, preferred a different breed of official than had Bludov. Miliutin's carefully balanced criticism of his ministry's famine relief programs in the region between St. Petersburg and Moscow first brought him to Stroganov's attention and, when the Count left his post in late 1841, he recommended Miliutin to Perovskii as a young man with unusual administrative gifts. A brief acquaintance convinced Perovskii that Stroganov had been correct; just over a year later, he entrusted Miliutin with an important new agency.[61] At age twenty-four, Miliutin thus took on the headship of the Economic Department's Provisional Section for the Reorganization of Municipal Government and Economy and was assigned to examine the economic and administrative structures in the Empire as a first step to preparing plans for renovating Russia's nearly defunct system of municipal government.[62] This work drew him directly into the autocratic legislative process. For the next several years he carried on a complex series of legislative negotiations with Perovskii and the State Council which produced the Statute on the Reform of St. Petersburg's Municipal Administration in 1846.

Had they remained faithful to Russia's bureaucratic traditions, Miliutin and his Provisional Section might have drafted nothing but proposals for minor adjustments in Russia's administrative apparatus. Yet despite his youth and inexperience, or, perhaps, because of them, Miliutin eventually produced a broad study of urban social and economic conditions in Russia and used the Provisional Section as a base from which to develop more important reform proposals.[63] To succeed, he needed investigators able to break with the formalism of Russia's administrative tradition and think in broader terms than were common in the St. Petersburg bureaucracy. Such men must be willing to ask questions that most bureaucrats feared to ask and to report corruption and incompetence without regard for the reputations of senior provincial officials. They had to possess the tenacity to ferret out evidence about such failings when local authorities proved uncooperative, and they had to be willing to remain away from the capital long enough to succeed. It required more than a decade to complete the ambitious task Miliutin had begun, but it provided him and his associates with a broader understanding of Russia's administrative processes. Even more important, it enabled him to assemble a cadre of talented officials within his agency to rival those whom Kiselev, Karneev, and Zablotskii had recruited into the Ministry of State Domains a few years before.

Although he criticized formalism and incompetence, Miliutin's efforts to deal with the administrative problems uncovered by his subordinates proved that he had not yet formulated broader solutions to the growing crisis in Russia's administration. He held a broad commission to draft a reform of Russia's municipal government institutions. Yet he shied away from doing so and allowed his preliminary studies in late

1842 and early 1843 to convince him that urban life was too varied and complex to fit any general administrative rules. Like his mentor Perovskii, he at first thought only of adjusting Russia's administrative apparatus to achieve the ideal of a well-ordered, finely tuned executive machine and narrowed his reform goals as a result.[64] At first determined to streamline the administration, not transform it, Miliutin could not formulate new and effective solutions to the problems that confronted him in Russia's cities, and he could not yet envision changes in the very concept of administration itself.[65] Anxious to postpone concrete attempts to transform provincial administration, Miliutin turned his attention to St. Petersburg, although he continued to send agents of special commissions into the provinces.

Beginning in the fall of 1843, Miliutin's efforts to draft a new municipal statute for St. Petersburg demonstrated the traditional limitations in his views about administration and government at that point as well as some modest innovations. Not satisfied with data obtained through usual sources, he consulted directly with elected city officials to learn how St. Petersburg's administrative agencies might be made more effective.[66] Sharing Zablotskii's faith in codification, he and his staff assembled all the materials available in central government offices about St. Petersburg, studied them, and prepared a thorough critique of earlier efforts to reform the city's government. By the end of 1843, he had assembled overwhelming evidence that the city's administration was a morass of incompetence, tangled lines of authority, and deeply rooted corruption. Such discoveries were hardly new, nor were his solutions.[67] He proposed to instill a sense of civic responsibility in elected city officials, an obviously difficult task when they were surrounded by an army of corrupt civil servants.[68] Then he defined more precisely the responsibilities of elected officials, broadened the base of class representation in St. Petersburg's central administration, and clarified administrative lines of authority.[69]

The provisions of Miliutin's reform proposals that Perovskii laid before the State Council in June 1844 have been discussed elsewhere and need not be reiterated here.[70] Like his conclusions about the renovation of city government in Russia, they remained quite traditional except on the question of taxation, where he opposed class privilege and championed state interest. During the 1820s and 1830s, the value of real estate in Russia's capital had soared. When he found that it was not reflected in the city's tax assessments, Miliutin hastened in mid-1843 to institute St. Petersburg's first property reassessment in more than two decades. As he uncovered cases of outright tax evasion among the city's aristocratic dwellers, he more than doubled their tax bills.[71] In reply, St. Petersburg's great lords immediately branded him an enemy of the aristocracy, and he bore that scar for the rest of his public life.[72] His challenge to noble class privilege became the main source of dispute between the Ministry of Internal Affairs and the State Council when it discussed his proposals for a new municipal statute late in 1844.

If Miliutin's reassessment of the properties of St. Petersburg's noblemen earned him their enmity, his plans for administrative reform drew the wrath of the city's merchant community when he sought their comments before submitting his proposals to the State Council. Such consultation with public opinion outside the bureaucracy had not been attempted since Catherine II's much-heralded Legislative Commission had failed in 1767. Yet far from acclaiming his efforts to encourage debate about important reform issues in their city, St. Petersburg's merchants rejected any attempt to regularize its administration, on the grounds that it violated traditional practice. Miliutin's proposals, they insisted, stood against the principles of autocracy and the "spirit of the Russian people," and even violated the fundamental laws of the Russian Empire.[73]

Although Miliutin's efforts to consult public opinion departed from autocratic legislative tradition, the merchants' opposition ensured its failure. Their rejection led him to conclude that only competent and far-seeing officials, backed by the authority of Russia's autocrat, could neutralize class opposition to change. Miliutin still carried that view to his work on the Great Reforms some fifteen years later. Rather than seek support among those segments of the nobility who were sympathetic to emancipation, he insisted that aristocratic participation in the Editing Commissions' work be minimized because he thought it unreasonable to expect those with a material stake in the old order to support its reform.[74]

Russia's senior statesmen shared Miliutin's desire to make St. Petersburg's administration more effective at the State Council hearings in October 1844, and they readily approved his plans to clarify administrative lines of authority and induce better elected officials to serve the city.[75] They opposed his efforts to establish any effective all-class decision-making bodies, insisted that the nobility have a decisive voice in the capital's affairs, and attempted to exclude some 3,000 of the city's smaller property holders from effective participation in its government.[76] It was a tribute to Miliutin's budding skill in guiding draft legislation through the higher reaches of the ministerial administration that he was able to strike a compromise with the Empire's senior statesmen on these issues.[77] The new St. Petersburg Municipal Statute gave representation to all classes on the General City Council, the capital's chief administrative policy-making body. In return, Miliutin had to watch the city's Administrative Council, the body that controlled tax levies and property assessments, become weighted heavily in favor of its noble residents.[78]

As it emerged from the State Council on February 13, 1846, the St. Petersburg Municipal Statute represented a compromise that served as a prototype for the municipal reform statute of 1870. Miliutin's achievement also had a broader significance because he had begun to use his Provisional Section as a testing ground for those young officials whose integrity, intelligence, and efficiency drew them to his attention. Miliutin's agency became another nucleus in the bureaucracy from which cadres of enlightened bureaucrats emerged to play a major role in planning the Great Reforms. Perhaps equally important, Miliutin's Municipal Statute provided him with rare experience in the autocratic legislative process. Of all those enlightened bureaucrats who drafted the Great Reforms, he was the only one with practical training in preparing reform legislation and guiding it through the upper reaches of the Russian administration. While others among his friends and colleagues boasted broader knowledge about local needs and conditions only Miliutin actually had taken a serious part in the legislative process that was so important for drafting and implementing change in Russia.

The conclusions that Miliutin drew from his experience in the 1840s embodied many of the positive and negative features of the enlightened bureaucrats' attitudes toward some of the most critical questions of the Great Reform era. To what extent should public opinion be consulted about reform legislation? What interaction should there be between officials, the autocrat, and Russia's privileged elite in the reform process? What motives should guide the state in fostering social transformation in Russia? The enlightened bureaucrats' responses to these vital questions had much of their genesis in Miliutin's experiences with the autocratic legislative process in the mid-1840s, although there were other factors that also influenced their views. Perhaps the most important among them was respect for the law. These men insisted that the law must control the exercise of power, and that power, capriciously applied, was one of the greatest blemishes upon the face of Russia at mid-century. Even though their opportunities were limited, they began to study Russia's laws, catalogue their faults, and plan ways to replace arbitrary authority with a rule of law during the latter half of Nicholas I's reign. Sergei Ivanovich Zarudnyi, a young man whom Panin thought the model state official, led the way in that endeavor.

Sergei Zarudnyi and Russia's Laws

In the Russia of Nicholas I, the absolute power of the Emperor reflected downward through all levels of society. If the Emperor's will, in theory, governed the acts of those below him, the same applied for those chief adjutants—his ministers—who spoke in his name. Such arbitrariness was even more deeply ingrained in the fabric of Russian society because noblemen possessed absolute authority over their serfs and brought that cast of mind into the bureaucracy. This was especially true of Russia's courts, where those who administered justice and the law usually were of noble background and were accustomed to exercising their unfettered will from birth. True justice, therefore, had become relatively rare by the 1830s and 1840s. Remarked one observer, "Russia . . . resembled a lake, in the depths of which great fish devoured the smaller ones, while near the surface everything was calm and glistened smoothly, like a mirror."[79] Of course Russian statesmen knew what went on in the depths of the lake, but, because the autocrat's jealousy about his prerogatives was nowhere more evident than in the dispensation of the law, they thought in terms of adjustments, not broader reforms.

If the law originated with the person of the ruler, then any effort to interpret it implied an undercutting of the autocrat's authority. For that reason, Russian rulers were particularly insistent that judges and other legal officials should administer the law, never interpret it. Especially after Speranskii made the law available in digest form, judicial officials were expected to apply it in the same manner as other civil servants applied other sorts of regulations. This was merely an instance of that more general phenomenon in which, as the French scholar Michel Crozier has shown, decisions must be made at the locus of power in any bureaucratic structure and, the more extreme its centralization, the higher the point in the hierarchy where decisions must be made.[80] If autocrats were to remain the only source of law, then they must preserve all power to make law in their hands alone. "Only the lawgiver, as the figure representing in her person all of society and holding all powers in her hands, has the right to make laws," Catherine II had written in her *Nakaz*. "There is nothing more dangerous," she warned, "than the general dictum that one must take into account the spirit of the law and not hold strictly to its letter."[81]

Because those who dispensed justice in Russia were to be no more than administrators of laws handed down by an absolute sovereign, they became abject agents who implemented, with mechanical precision, what they assumed was the Emperor's will, and gave little or no thought at all to true justice. One of Zarudnyi's contemporaries described an extreme instance of this way of thinking in his reminiscences about the Nicholas era:

A gendarme [regarded by the Emperor as a direct extension of his own person] appeared in the chamber [of justice] and urgently

59

demanded the execution of the instructions which he presented. The President [of the Chamber of Justice] immediately fell to thinking: "What was to be done?" After this, he ordered all the cases to be brought from the chancellery. Then he took one case, and raising it to his eyes, or, perhaps more accurately, to his nose, he declared: "Sustain the decision of the court," and laid [the papers relating to] this case to his right. Then he took another case and, repeating the process, declared: "Overturn the decision of the court." Then, with these motions, he rapidly began placing cases to the left and to the right, calling out: "Sustain! Overturn!" and so forth. When this was finished, the gendarme departed with the reports and all the cases in the Chamber of Justice had been decided.[82]

Even though justice itself had been poorly served, the will of the Emperor was fulfilled to the letter.

By the 1840s, the dispensation of justice in Russia had been reduced to a series of formulae which, ideally, could and should be applied without question, as Count Panin continued to insist that interpreting the law was irrelevant, even dangerous. Interpretive law texts were nonexistent, and the textbook of Russian law remained the *Digest of the Laws* itself. Not until 1845 did Professor D. I. Meier offer Russia's first university course on Russian civil law at the University of Kazan.[83] To study the law in Russia during the reign of Nicholas I meant to learn the *Digest of the Laws* and to apply its prescriptions just as any other set of administrative regulations might be applied. Russians who studied the theory of law studied it only in the abstract and only as it applied to legal systems in other countries.

To study Russian law itself—to begin to understand it and to learn its conflicts and inconsistencies—it was necessary to go to the source of its dispensation. This was the Consultation in the Ministry of Justice, where legal decisions were reviewed as part of a process by which that ministry prepared recommendations about disputed cases that had been brought before the Ruling Senate. Yet it was a difficult task to study the laws in the restricted environment of the Consultation because most who served there saw little difference between themselves as bureaucrats administering the law and officials in other ministries administering other affairs of state. No less than any other agency, the Ministry of Justice was staffed by *chinovniki* whose main concern was to move papers from one office to another.[84]

Sergei Zarudnyi's outlook differed sharply from his colleagues in the Ministry of Justice, and he became one of the first to study Russian laws at their source. Like Zablotskii and Miliutin, Zarudnyi came from impoverished noble roots and, again like them, he grew up in the country in intimate contact with serf life.[85] Although poor, his elders were well acquainted with the ideas of the Enlightenment, and books were his father's greatest passion. From his parents, Zarudnyi learned French, Italian, German, and English, and spoke the first two languages fluently before he left home.[86] The eighteenth-century Zarudynis had carved out respectable careers in the Imperial Guards, and Sergei diverged from that tradition only slightly when he chose to enter the Naval Cadet Corps. A simple error on his birth certificate ended his dreams of a naval career and left him with no means to continue his education. Crushed by such poverty that he could not even afford tutors to help him prepare for entrance examinations, he went to the southwestern university city of Kharkov, where he had to make his own way at the age of fourteen.[87] He seemed determined to seize hold of destiny in order to rise above his poverty. "Life is in opposition to the dictates of fate," he wrote.[88]

Although he earned a degree in mathematics at the University of Kharkov,[89] Zarudnyi never abandoned his childhood passion for literature. Like Miliutin, he fell under the spell of German romanticism, and that sustained him in his poverty. Prompted to search for a deeper meaning in life, he found it in struggle—in struggle against the dictates of fate, in struggle against passions, the external forces. "External forces —they are my enemy," he confided to his diary. "I want to think, but external forces do not permit me." To triumph over external forces meant to conquer passions, and Zarudnyi sought this "high moment of our life" in science and abstract thought.[90] In 1842, he applied unsuccessfully for a position at Russia's new Pulkovo Observatory, and so, in a desperate attempt to support himself, he turned to the civil service.[91] The brother of a distant relative was director of the Ministry of Justice's Department and grudgingly gave him a position. On November 27, 1842, Zarudnyi became a *kollezhskii sekretar'* in the Ministry of Justice.[92]

Zarudnyi entered Russia's Ministry of Justice under the regime of Panin, whom one historian has called the "most gloomy and callous representative of the old bureaucratic system,"[93] but who, like Kiselev and Perovskii, prized education in his subordinates. However, Panin made no effort to spare educated young men the frustration of inconsequential chancery tasks and, in fact, used it to test their mettle. Like Miliutin and Zablotskii, Zarudnyi found his first years in St. Petersburg devoted to those deadening bureaucratic routines that contemporary sources cursed as "a kind of clerkish rot and ignorance."[94] Zarudnyi proved himself capable and, in less than six months, became the senior assistant to the Office Section Chief in his department.[95] From that position he was able to turn the system to his advantage, as his scholarly abilities and analytic mind earned him that expert status that was so

N. A. Miliutin

Sergei Zarudnyi

important for liberating talented young men from the lower depths of the bureaucratic hierarchy.

As Head of the Second Section of His Majesty's Own Chancery, Count Dmitrii Bludov decided, in 1843, to investigate how the processes of Russia's civil law worked in practice and requested Count Panin to assemble comments from a number of judicial officials throughout the Empire for that purpose.[96] As the reports came into the Ministry of Justice's central offices, Zarudnyi was assigned to read and excerpt them before sending them on to the Second Section. It was a menial duty that Zarudnyi himself later described as one which "resembled most closely that of a postman."[97] Nonetheless, he made much of what seemed to others, from their formalistic, rank-conscious perspective, an inconsequential task, and he became an expert on the deficiencies in Russia's civil law code. "I had absolutely no knowledge whatsoever about the laws in general, or about our laws in particular," he later confessed in describing his first years in the Ministry of Justice. "After [studying] these imperfections in the laws, I went on to study the laws themselves," he continued. "The more imperfections I found in our laws, the more I enjoyed studying them. This was my school."[98] And there probably was no better school in which to study Russia's laws at the time. Even students at the Imperial School of Jurisprudence were trained only to administer the law efficiently, in keeping with the Emperor's view that the autocrat alone could make or interpret it. Zarudnyi's new expertise was much broader than such students of jurisprudence possessed.

In January 1847, Zarudnyi became an Office Section Chief in his Ministry's civil section to replace M. Kh. Reitern, a young official who soon rose, under the patronage of Grand Duke Konstantin Nikolaevich, to became Minister of Finance in the 1860s.[99] Zarudnyi's new duties placed him under the direct supervision of Mark Liuboshchinskii, the Department's Director. Also from impoverished aristocratic roots, Liuboshchinskii had entered the civil service some four years before Zarudnyi, after graduating from St. Petersburg University with a degree in law.[100] A friend of Miliutin, Zablotskii, and Reitern, Liuboshchinskii brought Zarudnyi into the company of well-educated, progressive young officials who were just beginning to seek alternatives to the administrative adjustments their superiors espoused. As men who respected the law and, in Zablotskii's words, "sought to introduce justice into all spheres of Russian life,"[101] they must have found Zarudnyi, with his passion for searching out contradictions and other failings in Russia's civil laws, a stimulating addition to their circle. By this time, Zarudnyi's deep interest in the law had grown far beyond any narrow concern about its unquestioning application.[102] That summer, he went abroad to be treated for an eye malady and tried to confirm his idealized view of Western law by what he later called "the realization of my democratic ideals." In Paris, he expected to find "those masses among whom the understanding of true law overcomes greed, where freedom defends itself with publicity, [and] where the aspiration for truth receives its fullest expression."[103] He haunted the city's law courts, was entranced by the orations of Jules Favre and Berryer, and became convinced that *glasnost'* (publicity), in legal proceedings, constituted one of the most fundamental guarantees that justice would prevail.[104] Not until the 1860s did he question his faith and realize that publicity in legal proceedings could not, by itself, assure the triumph of justice.

When Zarudnyi returned to take up his new duties in his Ministry's Department that fall, his ability to prepare clear and precise legal reports quickly endeared him to Panin, who once reportedly exclaimed: "If, just once in my life, I could present a report, or write a proposal, in the manner of Zarudnyi, then I should think that my life had not been lived in vain."[105] Zarudnyi thus assured himself of influence in Panin's ministry by excelling in those very routines he despised. While a number of his friends were critical of the bureaucracy's excessive formalism, none penned a more caustic critique than he about those tasks that Panin's regime obliged him to pursue with such apparent dedication. His criticism was not published until more than a decade after his death, when his son arranged for its publication in the historical journal *Russkaia starina.* Yet it almost certainly circulated in manuscript among his closest friends during the late 1840s and early 1850s, and it may well have been the subject of those private discussions at Miliutin's lodgings that Prince D. A. Obolenskii described in his memoirs as ones in which "the service milieu and senior statesmen were subjected to bitter and derisive criticism."[106]

Zarudnyi formulated his criticism of the bureaucracy in terms of a brilliantly satirical "letter from an experienced bureaucrat of the 'forties to a junior colleague just entering the service,"[107] in which he set forth a series of rules to guide young officials toward success. "Begin with the ABCs,"[108] he counseled, in terms clearly reminiscent of Bludov's advice to his son in 1838 to study the "alphabet of service."[109] Bludov had defined such an alphabet as embodying "habit, love for precision, and subordination."[110] For Zarudnyi, it represented that intense degradation to which a junior official must subject himself if he hoped to succeed in Russia's service. "Learn by heart such expressions as 'Your Excellency,'" he urged his fictitious junior colleague. "Begin and end your comments with this phrase when you address your kind and generous superior."[111] But Zarudnyi offered more than a criticism of the self-degradation demanded from junior bureaucrats, and he criticized the entire civil service for its rigidity, favoritism, and incompetence:

Do not depend so much upon your talents as upon patronage [*protektsiia*]. In spite of all your abilities, seek to shelter yourself under the wing of a successful patron. If you have *protektsiia*, then you will be considered a genius, able to undertake any task, and you will advance rapidly. But if you do not have *protektsiia*, then you will be considered an utter fool, fit for nothing, and knowing nothing, and you will never prosper in the service. . . .

If you are diligent, but do not complain that you have a thousand and one things to tend to, then you will never rise in the opinion [of your superiors]. Complain that you are absolutely snowed under with work and that, while others are doing nothing, you must work day and night. Always take home a portfolio bulging with papers and, although you may be working on something else at home, say that you are working on department affairs.

Try to pile all departmental cases upon others and, at the same time, complain that they are dumping all the work on you . . . so that you will be regarded as an able, experienced, and hard-working civil servant. . . . The first question you should ask yourself when you are assigned a case to work on ought to be: "How can I get out of doing it?"

Never stand on the side of truth when stronger forces, standing on the side of falsehood (but taking refuge in legal forms) are arrayed against you. . . . Never pay anywhere near as much attention to the substance of cases as to the people involved in them. . . . Never speak precisely on the basis of a particular law, but speak vaguely about legal bases.[112]

Such was Zarudnyi's perception of the central bureauracy in general and the Ministry of Justice in particular. His bitterness was easily the most intense of any expressed by his friends and like-minded associates, for Zablotskii, Miliutin, and those young men who worked with them during the 1840s at least had the comfort of serving under superiors who favored modest adjustments in the broader framework of the Nicholas system. Zarudnyi and his colleagues in the Ministry of Justice labored beneath the heavy hand of a minister who raised that very bureaucratic formalism they so despised to the highest level of virtue in order to enhance his personal authority.

Despite his inner feelings, Zarudnyi used Panin's favor to rise to positions of greater influence in the Ministry of Justice. In late October 1849, he became senior juridical consultant in the Ministry's Consultation, where senior officials frequently consulted him about difficult legal questions.[113] Panin reportedly called him "a master of [his] craft"[114] and placed considerable faith in his judgment, even though Zarudnyi was far more innovative than Panin's ideal of a legal specialist "trained to follow the law and orders."[115] Indeed, Zarudnyi used his new position to assemble young men of outstanding talent and education and to train them in the law in a way that universities and the Imperial School of Jurisprudence could not. "Zarudnyi managed to organize within the Consultation an entire school in which he tested the skills of the most talented young jurists," recalled Dmitrii Shubin-Pozdeev, one of the young men who served under him at that time.[116] Zarudnyi thus used the Ministry of Justice's Consultation to marshal cadres of talented officials directly under his command in much the same manner as Nikolai Miliutin and Zablotskii had used their agencies in the Ministries of Internal Affairs and State Domains. By mid-century, each had assembled a small group of highly trained officials; together they controlled a body of knowledge and experience that made them very necessary resources to their superiors.

If the expectations of Panin, Kiselev, and Perovskii were to be realized, the bureaucratic cadres that Miliutin, Zablotskii, and Zarudnyi commanded were essential to these efforts. Zarudnyi thus pursued the path upon which Miliutin and Zablotskii had embarked a few years before, and he perhaps had even more impact on the procedures and standards of his agency then they. "By working himself harder than anyone else," Shubin-Pozdeev recalled, "Zarudnyi had the rare ability to spur them [his subordinates] not only to work in the bureaucratic sense, but . . . [to instill in them] a desire to draft not only conclusions, but to work out every question from every angle and within its proper historical context."[117] His first attempt to direct his new bureaucratic resources toward reform goals came in 1852. Bludov's work on Russia's civil code again provided him with the opportunity.

Throughout the 1840s, Panin raised numerous petty objections to those portions of Bludov's broader proposals for reform of Russia's civil code that he deemed direct attacks upon his position in the bureaucratic hierarchy or threats to his ministerial authority.[118] By 1852, these two senior statesmen had reached a bureaucratic stalemate, and, in an attempt to break the impasse, Nicholas I created a special Imperial Commission to reconcile their conflicts. As an expression of his continued support, the Tsar named Bludov its head and appointed Deputy Minister of Justice P. D. Illichevskii to represent Panin's position. In addition, there were senators A. F. Veimarn, R. M. Gubet, and M. M. Karniolin-Pinskii, as well as a representative from the Ministry of Justice's Consultation, who soon was replaced by Liuboshchinskii, by then Chief Procurator of the Senate's First Department. Liuboshchinskii named Zarudnyi as the committee's chief administrator.[119]

The Committee of 1852 represented both traditionalists and men who favored change. The views advocated by Veimarn and Gubet remain unclear, as do those which Liuboshchinskii's predecessor held during his brief tenure. Karniolin-Pinskii, who had become a Senator just the year before, first had worked with Speranskii in the Second Section. For more than a decade after he transferred to the Ministry of Justice, he had ardently seconded Panin's efforts to recruit talented, well-educated officials, and it was thought that he even could influence his master on occasion. At that moment, however, Karniolin-Pinskii was desperately trying to divorce a wife whose scandalous affairs had produced several unwanted offspring,[120] and his state of mind obviously was not suited to a critical analysis of Russia's civil laws. Nor was that of his colleague Illichevskii, also a protégé of Speranskii, who might have been expected to support reform. But his was a strange and confused mind which, only a few years later, fell prey to madness. One official found Illichevskii utterly bored by the petty tasks Panin heaped upon him but so unassertive that his only protest was to sign his name (which he had begun to abbreviate "Ill. . .") vertically rather than horizontally. He became obsessed with service decorations and spoke of little else.[121] Prince Meshcherskii served with him just a few years later, called him *"nothing* in the fullest meaning of the word," and remarked that "everyone knew that he *in no way* was capable of any thought whatsoever."[122] On those rare occasions when he attended the Senate or the State Council, Illichevskii sat in silence;[123] it seems that he served in much the same manner on the Committee of 1852.[124]

Bludov's voice thus became dominant on the committee. In January 1849, he had told the Emperor that Russia's civil laws demanded "radical transformation" and proposed the introduction of limited adversarial procedure, the use of attorneys (who would hold civil service rank), and the creation of justices of the peace to mediate minor civil disputes.[125] Yet like Kiselev and Perovskii, Bludov's innovations still centered on modifications of procedure. At no time did he propose broader reforms, nor did he ever contemplate challenging the administrative authority of autocracy.[126] Zarudnyi therefore was forced to work for a reform of Russia's civil laws within this very limited framework and to limit his efforts to technical improvements.[127]

Panin's resistance to reforms that might "undermine irreparably the system,"[128] and Bludov's determination to preserve the autocrat's administrative authority, thus confined Zarudnyi's role to one very similar to that which Miliutin and Zablotskii had played in their respective agencies a few years earlier. With no clear alternative to propose and, in any case, unable to implement his conviction that Russia required broader, more fundamental changes, Zarudnyi was reduced to following the path of administrative adjustment. He and his close friends already had concluded, however, that this was insufficient to achieve the sort of "renovation" that Russia required.

The Foundations of a New Service Ethic

From the moment they entered Russia's civil service, such senior Nicholaean statesmen as Panin and Bludov had held elite offices that had allowed them to believe that their "superior sensitivity and taste"[129] immediately could be put at their country's disposal for some worthwhile purpose. Furthermore, they, as well as Kiselev and Perovskii, possessed the supreme self-confidence born of educations based on the teachings of the Enlightenment and early sentimentalism that their enlightened minds could create a superior administrative order in the civil, diplomatic, or military bureaucracies of Russia. Such would not come, they realized, without grief and suffering, but, in their view, that very fact gave deeper meaning to life and reaffirmed their faith that the future somehow would be better than the present. Service to the state transcended individual desires within the context of their sentimentalist service ethic, for they believed they ought not judge the actions of a ruler who stood on a far higher plane than they.[130] Such elite officials gave a sense of purpose to their lives by serving Tsar and country. Because their wealth and high birth had secured them material comforts, they could afford the intellectual luxury of seeking life's deeper meanings, and they formulated their spiritual lives within the framework of a society that had made their daily lives comfortable and satisfying. Count Bludov could extol the "alphabet of service, which is not taught in universities ... and [which is] not elementary, so-called material knowledge,"[131] because such qualities ensured his high position.

Such young men as Miliutin, Zablotskii, and Zarudnyi faced a very different situation. Without serfs or estates, they, and a number of others with similar economic and educational backgrounds, set out to make bureaucratic careers for themselves in order to improve their lives. Although unusually well-educated and untypically energetic, they were not spared a number of painful years in the lower ranks of Russia's pettifogging clerical army before they rose to higher positions. As a consequence of the rigid service system Nicholas I imposed on Russia, their late adolescent years were devoted to the scribe's inky trade, not to those duties that had fostered the self-esteem of their Alexandrine predecessors. Miliutin and Zablotskii knew the boredom of inconsequential chancery work, while Zarudnyi, despite his university degree, was first assigned the menial clerical duty of summarizing reports. A number of their colleagues suffered similar experiences. Future state secretary and member of the Committee of Ministers V. P. Butkov actually devoted his first years as a civilian official in the War Ministry to becoming a living catalogue of his ministry's archives and was promoted five grades in the Table of Ranks in just three years as a reward.[132]

Rather than flattering their self-image and nourishing their aspirations, life in Russia's service in the 1830s and early 1840s crushed the young men who exchanged the security of their elite school classrooms for clerks' stools in offices buried deep within those great chanceries with which the architect Rossi so recently had adorned St. Petersburg. This stark reality pressed upon them from all sides; it condemned them to tasks they thought too menial for men of their elite educations, destroyed their dreams, and oppressed their spirits. Nikolai Miliutin once wrote that a "conflict between life and poetry" faced them,[133] a conflict in which, as his elder brother Dmitrii once reported from the army, everything was "totally at odds with my former conceptions, habits, and studies."[134] These young men could not insulate themselves from reality as did those who remained at the university to immerse themselves in the intellectual currents of the 1830s. For them, life had to take precedence over poetry. "Hard work and a sense of duty"[135] replaced idealism, and while they did not immediately make their peace with the hard reality of service life, they had to become reconciled to it. Periodic lapses into their old language of idealism no longer rang true as they left their world of dreams behind them.[136] For them, "literature" and "poetry" gave way to "politics" as the 1840s dawned.[137]

Just when these young men began to abandon their idealist concerns about beauty and truth in favor of pragmatic concerns, the idealism of their schoolmates who had shunned the bureaucracy was challenged in an equally painful manner. *"I do not know exactly, but something is wrong,"* one worried informant wrote to Count Benkendorf, and that warning led the Chief of Nicholas's Third Section to report that Russians were beginning to exhibit "a state of mind and feelings which is less propitious than at any time during the entire past fifteen years."[138] Benkendorf's apprehensions caused a number of Russia's intellectuals to cease writing; others were driven from their newly won university faculty posts because they failed to praise sufficiently the established order. For some of those who no longer could serve Russia with their pens, the bureaucracy offered a means of support, a refuge from the prominence they had gained as writers, and a limited opportunity to serve their country and its people.

In the moderate intelligentsia's search for havens during the 1840s, Perovskii played an important and unique role. "Perovskii liked to surround himself with individuals who had been educated in the university and were talented in scholarly and literary work," wrote one of his contemporaries,[139] while the novelist Mel'nikov-Pecherskii recalled that he "insisted it was necessary for any truly enlightened minister to conduct himself in such a manner."[140] Given the limited number of graduates emerging from Russia's elite schools and universities, Perovskii rightly viewed those well-educated intellectuals whom the Third Section so feared as an untapped source of talent. He offered them positions in his ministry just when they were seeking some means to withdraw from public view. The philologist Vladimir Dal', whom he named director of his personal chancellery, was merely the first among many.[141] During the next decade, Perovskii recruited Nikolai Nadezhdin, Ivan Aksakov, Ivan Turgenev, Count A. K. Tolstoi, Mikhail Saltykov-Shchedrin, Ivan Panaev, Aleksandr Herzen, and Nikolai Nekrasov, as well as Iuri Samarin, Konstantin Kavelin, Petr Redkin, Count Sollogub, and V. V. Grigor'ev.[142] Slavophiles, Westerners and even former political exiles all found places under his protection as he attempted, with considerable success, to employ their very obvious talents for Russia's welfare.

Perovskii's enlightened recruitment policies, combined with those of Kiselev in the Ministry of State Domains, made it possible to restore that exchange of ideas between the young men who had left their friends in Moscow's university and literary circles to enter Russia's service in the 1830s. This interchange was broadened by a new influx of young men from the Empire's elite schools and universities in the

1840s who, even more than the generation of Miliutin, Zablotskii, and Zarudnyi, felt impelled toward careers in government service. Romanticism had touched both groups but had produced very different effects. When combined with sentimentalism, it produced an exaltation of feeling that was poor preparation for the stark realities of a civil servant's life in St. Petersburg. The conflict between "poetry" and "politics" all but paralyzed Miliutin, Zarudnyi, Aleksandr Girs, and Konstantin Grot during their first year or two in the St. Petersburg bureaucracy, precisely because of the passivity that sentimentalism had instilled in them. Coupled with realism, however, romanticism produced a more positive affirmation of young Russians' abilities to act upon the world around them, and that was very much a part of the experience of those who entered the bureaucracy from Russia's elite schools in the 1840s. Sentimentalism had spawned passivity that could be overcome only at the cost of considerable emotional torment for such youths as Miliutin, Zablotskii, and Zarudnyi, but romanticism tinged with realism gave birth to an adoration of heroic deeds among the young men who followed them to St. Petersburg. They found positive heroes in the novels of Victor Hugo, James Fenimore Cooper, Sir Walter Scott, and, most of all, Alexandre Dumas,[143] and that impelled them to seek a more active course for their lives. As V. R. Zotov, soon to become a civilian official in the War Ministry, wrote in 1840, "Glory is our heart's desire/ To serve our country and our Tsar!"[144] Mixed with readings of Hegel and, later, the writings of the French utopian socialists, such adoration of heroic action led this new "generation" of young officials to become concerned about social problems and to advocate confronting them through positive action.

The generation of the 1840s was disposed by their school-boy intellectual experiences to think about Russia's problems in more action-oriented terms; in the university, their teachers urged them further along that path. Within the context of the Hegelian ideal that Timofei Granovskii, Petr Redkin, and Konstantin Kavelin lauded in their lectures at Moscow University, students came to think of change as a phenomenon taking place over time, and they thus rejected the need for accepting passively that existing order which had been so much a part of the sentimentalist service ethic. Under the influence of their professors' interpretations of Hegel, they began to believe that a heightened consciousness, gained through study and scientific inquiry, could enable them to take part in the great universal process of change, and that in turn affirmed their ability to improve the quality of life in Russia.[145] Their new convictions were reinforced at the Sunday gatherings that Granovskii's close friend Kavelin held for his students. Kavelin passionately argued against serfdom, and the effectiveness of his pleadings can best be judged by noting that a number of those who attended his Sunday gatherings appeared among the liberal minorities on those provincial committees that discussed the problems of emancipation in 1858.[146] At the same time, V. S. Poroshin opened to those who attended his lectures about political economy at St. Petersburg University the teachings of the French utopian socialists, which elevated the dignity of the individual above all else and held the well-being of all members of society, not the interests of a privileged elite, to be of paramount importance.[147]

Adolescent intellectual experiences that led the young men of the 1840s to think in broader terms about society and its welfare were reinforced by formal educations that focused more concretely on Russian reality and prepared them more directly for careers in government service. Dmitrii Miliutin could remark with considerable truth that "we, Moscow youths, had very vague notions in general about service affairs,"[148] because life in Russia's service did not consume his teachers' and classmates' attention. There was more concern with service affairs in the school experiences of Miliutin's contemporaries who attended St. Petersburg's elite schools, but, even there, a number of wealthy young nobles did not think exclusively in those terms. Until the 1840s, Russia's more wealthy noble youths thought it important to have been in state service, but they felt it necessary to devote no more than a few years to such tasks before they could retire *cum dignitate* to pursue other interests. "In the family into which I was born, it was considered a matter of class honor from generation to generation for young noblemen to devote their young adult years to military service," wrote Konstantin Veselovskii. "Because of this," he continued, "they entered the army not for the purpose of making it a lifelong profession, but so that, after spending a few years in it, they could retire with at least the rank of major . . . and, with a feeling of having done his duty, each could return to the bosom of his peaceful estate."[149] By contrast, government service became an all-absorbing concern for most students toward mid-century. "Hearing not only at school, but also at home, about the achievements of our predecessors, we let our thoughts dwell upon what was for us the most understandable and attractive side of our future service careers," Konstantin Arsen'ev recalled in remembering his student days at the Imperial School of Jurisprudence.[150] Unlike some of the youth of the 1830s, these students hastened into the service, as Valuev once explained, "so as not to be delayed in reaching the much-desired rank of *statskii sovetnik.*"[151]

The young men who entered the agencies of Zablotskii, Miliutin, and Zarudnyi in St. Petersburg during the mid- to late 1840s had a sense of elite identity that was even more pervasive than that of the men

71

under whom they first chose to serve, and this provided them with a more secure self-image once they had launched their careers. In an effort to improve the quality of provincial civil servants, the Emperor Nicholas had decreed in 1839 that university or elite school graduates must serve at least three years in the provinces before they could be eligible for positions in the capital. Only the handful who had graduated with distinction were exempted from this requirement, and, therefore, those young men who began their careers in St. Petersburg after 1840 had the sense of belonging to a particularly select group.[152] Feelings of eliteness were enhanced for graduates of the Lyceum at Tsarskoe Selo and the Imperial School of Jurisprudence by the intense loyalties which they held toward their classmates and their *alma mater.* "In their midst developed those elements of simple brotherly unanimity, exemplary comradeship, which bound them together after graduation and throughout their lives," explained Aleksei Iakhontov, who added that "there developed among all *litseisty* [Lyceum graduates] a love for their school and for Tsarskoe Selo as their childhood home."[153] *Litseisty* loved their school and forgave it its faults. "It is true that the Lyceum requires changes," Golovnin once confessed. "But as a *litseist,*" he added, "I do not want to lay a hand upon our beloved *alma mater.* Let others do so after I am gone."[154]

The ties that bound *litseisty* as youths endured into later life. Romantic poems written by adolescents about to enter the bureaucracy glorified their common bonds of camaraderie and shared youthful passions:

> And do remember when, bewailing youth,
> The days we spent in Lyceum's garden,
> When you serenely blossomed
> And life's grief was yet unknown.
> M. Longinov (1840)[155]

> With new strength cement our beauteous union,
> Preserve our comradely vows
> In sacred communion.
> N. P. Semenov (1841)[156]

Friendships formed at the Lyceum became life-long commitments, and the impact of such school ties on the articulation of state policy later in the nineteenth century remains one of those fascinating questions yet to be studied by historians. Such bonds united the conservative D. A. Tolstoi and the more progressive A. V. Golovnin, M. Kh. Reitern, and A. K. Girs, who diverged sharply on political questions but joined in celebrations held on October 19th every year to commemorate the Lyceum's opening. For that day they set aside political animosities to be rejoined in those ties established during their long-ago adolescence.

Like the *litseisty*, the *pravovedy*, graduates from the Imperial School of Jurisprudence, were acutely conscious of shared comradely experiences which remained treasured memories long after they had gone into the civil service. More than four decades after his graduation, the *pravoved* V. V. Stasov captured the intensity of those feelings when he wrote the following reminiscences:

> Our class, our microcosmic world, was for me, as for many of my comrades, something that was forever dear, treasured, and alluring. . . . All my love, all my sympathy, and interests . . . were transferred to the school and to my classmates. I found there much of that which home and family could not provide. . . . This was a life among equals with comrades devoted to a common task and occupation. . . . The conversations and arguments, the lively exchanges of ideas about things we had just read, regardless of whether they were mild and friendly or rude and hostile, were attractive to youths and endlessly treasured in their memories. These were our first guideposts. . . . Here our opinions were formed and our convictions strengthened.[157]

For *pravovedy*, their school became their *alma mater* in the broadest sense. With their classmates they formed close and lasting fraternal ties based on shared emotional, spiritual, and physical gratifications, and these helped to ease their transition from school to service under Panin's stern regime. Also like the *litseisty*, their common bonds defined to some extent later service relationships. "For him, a comrade from the School [of Jurisprudence] is something like a spiritual brother, who on all occasions, including promotions in service, should be given unquestioned preference over others," explained one observer about the *pravoved* Konstantin Pobedonostsev after he had risen to become one of the most influential men in Russia.[158]

The *pravovedy* thus comprised a corps of experts trained in the law, very conscious of their elite status, and bound together by firm and enduring ties. Some became a part of Zarudnyi's "school" in the Ministry of Justice. Others formed a body of reformist opinion in the Moscow Departments of the Senate, which were less oppressed by Panin's regime than were judicial agencies in St. Petersburg. Still others transferred to different ministries in order to advance their careers more rapidly. Prince Dmitrii Obolenskii and Pavel Glebov moved into the Naval Ministry to join the reformist *konstantinovtsy* in the mid-1850s. Some of their classmates later transferred to the Ministry of Internal

Affairs to serve under Miliutin or to the Ministry of State Domains to serve under Zablotskii. However and wherever they served Russia, *pravovedy* remained faithful to the admonition that their school's patron Prince Oldenburgskii had given at its first graduation ceremony to "preserve that fervent desire with which you long to show your limitless thanks for the inestimable grace of Our August Ruler who gave you such a great means to prepare yourselves for the service."[159] Many also endeavored to win influence and high status as rewards for excelling in their Emperor's service.

When these young men left their schools for the chanceries of St. Petersburg, they did not remain as isolated as Miliutin, Zarudnyi, Zablotskii or those others who had gone into the bureaucracy in the 1830s with elite educations as their only instrument for advancement. Entry into St. Petersburg's impersonal bureaucratic world was eased for the youth of the 1840s because their school ties helped them to obtain civil service positions from older graduates who had risen to head offices and departments. A. K. Girs, who left the Lyceum in 1835, was followed into the Ministry of Internal Affairs in the 1840s by A. V. Golovnin and D. A. Tolstoi, both of them future ministers. Konstantin Grot, who entered the Ministry of State Domains in 1838, was followed by Nikolai Garting and several others. Similar movements can be seen in the War Ministry during the early 1840s[160] and the Admiralty in the early 1850s,[161] where older comrades opened the way for younger ones.

Entrance into the civil service was facilitated further for these young men because Miliutin, Zablotskii, and Zarudnyi had created an institutional apparatus which enabled them to rise more easily, and a number deliberately entered these agencies because their directors were reputed to recognize talent and merit more quickly.[162] This new generation of civil servants was not obliged to struggle for the recognition that would lift them above the gray clerical mass in the central bureaucracy during their first years in Russia's service. Elite school graduates of the 1840s, therefore, did not spend their first years as officials in bitter conflict with the system of which they had become a part but, instead, worked on resolving administrative problems they thought important. Thus, when Nikolai Vtorov entered the Ministry of Internal Affairs in 1844, he found, in sharp contrast to the bitter experiences of Miliutin, Zablotskii, and Zarudnyi, "a friendly and like-minded circle of young men from the universities and lycées who dealt with administrative questions not from a paper-shuffling, purely formalistic, or casuistic perspective, but who sought to see the heart of the matter at hand, trying when possible to decide questions on well-informed bases and to institute a clear-cut system under which ... [they sought to reach] more solid and broadly based decisions on any given question."[163]

Young men such as Vtorov already were predisposed to think about society and its welfare, for they were trained above all to serve the state and their Emperor. Like their predecessors, they sought models in the service, but they were not obliged to emulate, for want of anything better, those senior statesmen whose sentimentalist service ethic had proved so inhospitable for Zablotskii and his friends a decade before. Vtorov, his friends, and associates found far better models in Zablotskii, Zarudnyi, and Miliutin, whose economic status and career aspirations were similar to their own. "All of us, or almost all of us," Konstantin Arsen'ev once remarked, "regarded the service from the point of view of personal success or personal advantage."[164]

The elite school graduates of the late 1830s and 1840s also were closer to each other in intellectual outlook than Zablotskii, Miliutin, or Zarudnyi had been to their Alexandrine mentors. Both stood relatively close to each other in the service hierarchy and worked closely together to resolve administrative problems and study conditions in Russia. Although the men of the 1830s had by then become office section chiefs and department heads, they did not allow rank and position to separate them from their like-minded subordinates. Young Aleksandr Shumakher later remembered that "younger officials with higher educations began to exchange opinions and to consult with each other on more serious questions that were being dealt with by their various office sections. In doing so, they sought to establish clear principles based on reason and knowledge in the decision of such matters."[165]

These men shared a belief that their knowledge could be used for the benefit of Russia and that this goal could be achieved within the framework of the bureaucracy in which they served. They also shared what Prince Dmitrii Obolenskii once called an "incomprehensible, firm hope that the present order could not continue for very long and that better days soon must come."[166] This was particularly important because experience already had shown such men as Miliutin and Zablotskii that most government officials still were abysmally ignorant about the true state of Russian social and economic life, and they had concluded that progressive officials ought to make a broader knowledge of Russian conditions their first priority. This simply had seemed good administrative practice at first, but the influx into their offices of well-educated young men who believed that the acquisition of such knowledge could become part of a universal process by which they might participate in evolutionary change added a dynamic dimension to their studies. Rather than collect data mechanistically, they began to press for reform itself, as was evident in the shifting priorities of Miliutin's Municipal Section. By 1848, his investigators no longer merely gathered information about abuses of power and administrative malpractices in provincial towns but actually attempted to curtail them.[167]

St. Petersburg's chanceries constituted only one arena in which the interchange of ideas between progressive officials took place during the 1840s. Their discussion was broadened further by their many social encounters. The 1840s and early 1850s saw several interconnected circles emerge in St. Petersburg, and the meetings of bureaucratic colleagues in these informal surroundings were important for broadening their ideas, developing their views about change, and expanding the circle of men able to bring specialized knowledge about Russian conditions to bear on the issues of reform and renovation. As these circles developed, they came to shelter most of the men who drafted the Great Reforms legislation. During the difficult decade that Russians lived through between Europe's revolutions of 1848 and the Crimean War, these men elaborated upon the new service ethic that was beginning to emerge from the agencies of Zablotskii, Miliutin, and Zarudnyi. They reached a broader view of what reform ought to be and how it could be implemented within Russia's conservative, and increasingly outdated, political system.

chapter 3

Forces Assemble

"These young men worked, studied, and read, and they looked upon the pointless, empty life of high society with contempt. . . . [They were sustained by] some incomprehensible hope that the present order could not continue for very long and that better days soon must come."

Prince Dmitrii Obolenskii

During the 1840s, Russia's moderate intellectuals developed a new awareness of their obligation to pursue knowledge, not for itself, but for the benefit of society. This so-called return to reality freed them from those ivory towers to which their intellectual wanderings had confined them during the 1830s and returned them to the mainstream of pragmatic affairs. In those central government offices most concerned with learning more about Russian economic, social, and legal conditions, Miliutin, Zablotskii, and Zarudnyi urged their subordinates to break down those mountains of official papers generated by the bureaucracy's dedication to the rituals of formalistic administration in order to better understand the complexities of Russian life. Having risen to more prestigious positions as directors of office sections, they insisted that the officially accepted portrait of life outside St. Petersburg and Moscow was inaccurate because it had been painted by subordinates bent on pleasing their superiors. A decade spent in the Russian bureaucracy had convinced them that such administrative adjustments as Kiselev, Perovskii, and Panin had advocated no longer could suffice, and they urged responsible officials to learn more about Russia's economic life, social problems, and the failure of her laws to function properly in order to understand the increasingly complex situation the Empire faced as mid-century approached. Such knowledge, they thought, could provide a basis for social and economic changes, although they did not yet perceive the broader dimensions of these changes. During the last decade of Nicholas's reign, their increasingly close relationship with new elite school and university graduates helped to clarify their view. Together, moderate intellectuals and progressive bureaucrats interracted to consider the most fundamental dilemmas of progress and develop the reform view that became so fundamental to the genesis of Russia's Great Reform legislation. Above all, they needed to direct the forces of social change on a positive course and broaden the political role of newly emergent economic groups in order to establish a broader political base for autocracy. This had to be accomplished despite the inevitable opposition of nobles who held high government offices and wielded great political influence.

The return to reality that moderate intellectuals and progressive officials shared during the last decade of the Nicholas era, coupled with their common commitment to change, established a reconciliation between them which partly counteracted the better-known "parting of ways" that had occurred when the paths of progressive opinion and state authority had diverged after 1825.[1] "How could I be lured into government service under the political conditions which prevailed at that time?" asked the young Westerner Boris Chicherin in describing the vast gulf he perceived between the government and public opinion at mid-century. "To become the direct instrument of a government that mercilessly oppressed every thought and all enlightenment and which, as a consequence, I detested from the bottom of my soul," he continued, "was the prospect that lay before me. I turned away from it with indignation."[2] By contrast, experience taught the Slavophile Ivan Aksakov that Chicherin's preference for abandoning the government's path could be even less desirable than service itself. Aksakov retired after two years in the bureaucracy rather than perform the duties he found distasteful; however, he soon realized that his conscience would not permit him to remain apart, even though he, like Chicherin, might have preferred to do so. As he confessed in a remarkably candid letter to Miliutin:

> Having retired from the service, I found myself in a rather unpleasant position. In the first place, it was necessary for me to live . . . from the labor of my serfs. In the second place, any sort of civic activity in literature was impossible under the present conditions. Finally, I now know that I can be neither a serf-owning landlord nor a speculator. I have been forced to recognize that even though one struggles unsuccessfully against the falsehood of contemporary life, one still is obligated, as an honorable man, to carry the heroic struggle to its last extremity.[3]

Aksakov's statement was important for a number of reasons, not the least of which were his desire to hold a useful civic position and his refusal to live from his serfs' labor, even though many of his associates continued to do so. Just two years earlier, in fact, the great revolutionary exile Aleksandr Herzen had managed to sell his serfs at a substantial profit. With the advice of Baron James Rothschild, he reaped lucrative profits from investments in Parisian real estate and American bonds, and became precisely the sort of speculator to whom Aksakov referred.[4] Aksakov's remarks also were noteworthy because they embodied all those diverse elements that comprised the outlook of a man of the 1840s. In his dedication to heroic struggle's "last extremity," he displayed the sort of commitment to positive action that helped bridge the gap between the passivity of Russian intellectuals in the 1830s and their involvement in the reform debate of the late 1850s.

While Chicherin shunned civic action by remaining at Moscow University to work on his doctoral dissertation until 1857,[5] Aksakov sought Miliutin's intercession to find another position in the Petersburg bureaucracy, where he hoped "to serve good and truth with all the talent of my soul."[6] Although each dealt in different ways with his hatred of Nicholas's oppressive authority, both were closely associated with those intellectual circles that shaped the outlook of some of the leading figures among Russia's intelligentsia during the Nicholas era. In Moscow, the Herzen and Stankevich circles were instrumental in the ideological development of those intense young men who emerged as Westerners and Slavophiles in the 1840s, while the circles of Ivan Panaev, Andrei Kraevskii, and, to a lesser degree, Mikhail Petrashevskii, were important in the intellectual life of St. Petersburg a brief decade later. True, there were those like Ivan Turgenev who, in his tale about "Hamlet of Shchigrovskii District," cursed such intellectual circles as "a destruction of any original development [and] . . . a disgraceful substitute for society, women, and real life,"[7] but for many passionate, thinking young men they were, as Chicherin later wrote, "supportive, encouraging, and stimulating." Chicherin readily admitted that these groups had their faults, but he saw no alternative as mid-century approached. "What was one to do when they wouldn't let people out into the open air?" he asked. "These were the only lungs with which Russian thought, being squeezed from all sides at the time, had to breathe at all."[8] So great was the impact of these groups on the intellectual life of Russians that any number of studies about the intelligentsia during the 1830s and 1840s have been formulated in terms of those circles which dominated the lives of their members.[9] The ideas they discussed have been often and well studied and need not occupy our attention here. More important, there were less-studied circles in St. Petersburg that were influenced in important ways by these more illustrious groups.

Progressive Bureaucrats and St. Petersburg's Circles

St. Petersburg's lesser circles did not command such broad loyalties as did those of Herzen, Ogarev, and Stankevich during the 1830s or that of Belinskii and Panaev in the 1840s. Nor did the views of the members of these circles find expression in major journals, as did those of the more famous *Sovremennik* circle. Their members did not confront those cursed questions of the era with such intensity, and their ranks did not include those towering intellectual figures who directed the development of progressive and radical Russian opinion during the 1840s and 1850s. Their members shared interests that were only slightly less binding nonetheless. Concerned with western ideas, literature, and politics, they conceived of change as an evolutionary process, and they advocated reform, not revolution. These broadened views of reform were of major consequence in determining the character of the Great Reforms.

These lesser circles are difficult to study and even more difficult to discuss in the terms that historians have applied to their more illustrious counterparts. Far less conscious of their historical importance, their members were more modest, and intellectual debate was not the central focus of their lives. Because much of their time and attention was taken up with governmental affairs, almost none of these men kept diaries, and very few ever wrote memoirs. "There were times," Miliutin's elder brother Dmitrii once wrote, "when I contemplated keeping a diary in order to remember everything that was somewhat noteworthy that I happened to observe or in which I was myself a participant. But I managed to accomplish this undertaking only . . . at odd moments," he confessed. "After a short-lived effort, I abandoned this attempt for lack of time."[10] Although most conscious of the need to leave a record for posterity, Dmitrii Miliutin began to keep a regular diary only in 1873, as he neared sixty. His brother Nikolai never did so, except during the brief weeks he spent with Zablotskii and Keppen in southern Russia during 1837. The same was true of Zarudnyi, and Zablotskii never made even a first attempt to begin a diary. Valuev, whose caustic remarks we cited at the beginning of this study, kept a lengthy diary between 1847 and 1884 but, before his death, destroyed most of the sections that related to the Nicholas era.[11]

These men also left few memoirs about those difficult years just before and during the Crimean War. Although the indefatigable Dmitrii Miliutin was an exception, he was out of St. Petersburg during most of the 1840s. In any case, he became so cautious about any discussion of reform questions as a professor at the General Staff War Academy toward the end of the decade that he instinctively transferred that circumspection to his memoirs so that they are less reliable about this period than others. Among other enlightened bureaucrats, only Aleksandr Golovnin wrote memoirs, but he emphasized the 1860s, not the 1840s.[12]

Such men were extremely reticent in their letters about matters of a private and intellectual nature. All lived and served in St. Petersburg, saw each other frequently, and had no reason to commit their disputes and discussions to paper. They had begun to occupy positions from which they could hope to influence state affairs and stood to lose a great deal if they roused the suspicion of their superiors or the police. Even when one among them left the capital on an official assignment, or traveled to the West, they avoided any written comment on broader questions of change or matters of an intellectual nature. There are no remarks about political or intellectual issues in the letters that Nikolai Miliutin sent home to friends during his visit to western Europe in 1845 and 1846.[13] The same was true of his lengthy correspondence with his close friend A. K. Girs, who often was away from St. Petersburg on official assignments during the mid-1840s.[14]

The paucity of the types of sources that have figured so prominently in studies about the leading circles of Moscow and St. Petersburg makes it especially difficult to examine those lesser circles in which progressive bureaucrats and moderate intellectuals congregated. Further, we do not have voluminous police reports about them as we do, for example, about the gatherings that Petrashevskii held at his lodgings at about the same time because these groups were careful not to attract the attention of the police. Nonetheless, even a limited discussion of these less visible groups can broaden our picture of the interchange between bureaucrats and moderate intellectuals that occurred during the 1840s and early 1850s as they discussed the ideas of the West, analyzed the failings of Russia's society and government, and grappled with the dilemmas of reform and change.

Like many young officials, Nikolai Miliutin at first lived a poor and lonely life, sharing two poorly heated rooms with a former schoolmate and trying to make ends meet on the miserly salary he received as a *gubernskii sekretar'* in the Ministry of Internal Affairs.[15] During his first year in the capital, his only friends were his elder brother Dmitrii (then a student at the General Staff War Academy) and Mikhail Leks, his kindly middle-aged superior in the ministry's Economic Department.[16]

Early in 1837, however, Miliutin moved to more spacious lodgings on the Ekaterinskii Kanal, and more friends began to gather more frequently at his rooms.[17] At first there was only Ivan Arapetov (another former schoolmate who later served with Miliutin on the Editing Commission), Zablotskii, Konstantin Arsen'ev (Zablotskii's immediate superior), and Grigorii Nebolsin, a statistician at the university. Consumed by romantic notions of comradeship—of which the declarations that Herzen and Ogarev made to each other on Sparrow Hills were not an overly extreme example[18]—they felt isolated during their first years in the capital and attempted to recreate their "schoolboy" circles as an antidote to the loneliness of their new lives. They met only for a few months before Miliutin and Zablotskii joined Keppen to study peasant life in Russia's southern provinces, and it would seem that their discussions centered mainly on service gossip and casual social matters.[19] At that point they still were dedicated to emulating their superiors rather than to seeking paths of their own.

When Miliutin returned, in mid-1838, from his year-long assignment in the South, his evening gatherings began to include a broader sampling of men of progressive views. Dmitrii Miliutin later recalled that his younger brother's long stay in the provinces in the company of Keppen and Zablotskii had left him more sober and that he had become seriously interested in economics, statistics, and problems of state administration.[20] Konstantin Veselovskii, later a member of the Academy of Sciences who struck up a friendship with Miliutin around 1840, recalled that the young men who came to his rooms debated a wide range of political, economic, judicial, and historical questions and discussed how they related to Europe and Russia. These young men were faithful readers of *Journal des Débats, Le Temps,* and *La Siècle,* and they were seriously interested in the parliamentary life of Louis-Philippe's France.[21] By the winter of 1846, Miliutin's weekly gatherings had begun to include members of the Petersburg intelligentsia as well. "In the evenings, I. P. Arapetov, A. P. Zablotskii, Count Ivan Petrovich Tolstoi, Liubimov, Kriukovskii, and other general acquaintances often assembled," Dmitrii Miliutin remembered. "To this intimate circle, others were added gradually," he continued. "Among their number, the most prominent was Nikolai Ivanovich Nadezhdin, with whom my brother Nikolai worked in editing *The Journal of the Ministry of Internal Affairs.* "[22] The former editor of the Moscow weekly *Teleskop,* Nadezhdin only recently had returned from the Siberian exile.

Dmitrii Miliutin remembered only that "there were absorbing discussions about scientific and artistic questions [and] these were always animated, often by a dash of humor or amusing stories," at his brother's lodgings.[23] But debate within Nikolai Miliutin's circle of friends had begun to center on more serious issues than his brother chose to recall. A. E. Tsimmerman, a young army officer who knew both brothers at the time, later wrote that "even during the reign of Nikolai Pavlovich, Dmitrii and, especially, Nikolai Miliutin, were well known for their liberal views," but he added that "the elder brother became frightened by this reputation and conducted himself with extreme caution."[24] The great geographer Petr Semenov, a distant relative and a close acquaintance, added that Dmitrii Miliutin was "the most cautious and circumspect"[25] of his family and feared that the discussions at his brother's lodgings might do harm to the military career he had pursued with such dedication for more than a decade.

There was, of course, good reason for Dmitrii Miliutin's excessive caution. By the mid-1840s, his brother's circle had become very much involved in criticisms of Russia's administration, even though they remained staunch defenders of autocracy. Zablotskii, perhaps the most influential member of the group after Miliutin himself, characterized their friends as "neither revolutionaries nor constitutionalists," but men who favored progress through orderly evolution within the framework of autocracy. Their belief in justice, hard work, and duty—those virtues in which, according to Zablotskii, "they saw not only the means without which it is impossible to improve one's position in society legitimately, but also a necessary requirement for the full enjoyment of life ... and a basic law of morality"—made them sharply critical of the bureaucratic processes in which all were involved.[26] The rare account left by Obolenskii, a *pravoved* who attended Miliutin's gatherings regularly, makes it even more clear that their discussions involved far sharper criticisms than the "absorbing discussions about scientific and artistic questions" which Dmitrii Miliutin later recalled. According to Obolenskii's recollections, written considerably earlier than Miliutin's:

> Service conditions and the highest-ranking statesmen were subjected to bitter and sarcastic criticism. Everyone came with his own anecdote to tell about his minister or director, and hearty laughter greeted the words of each speaker. At that time, liberal ideas did not, in general, have a defined form. Among political and economic works we preferred to read the new books: Proudhon, Fourier, Louis Blanc, and so forth. The French revolution of 1848 animated these young men even more, but this animation was purely platonic. It goes without saying that no one dreamed of standing in the ranks of overt revolutionaries. But, being unable to sympathize with that strict regime in which all society was held, especially beginning with the year 1848, these young men worked, studied, and read, and they looked upon the pointless, empty life of high society with contempt. Fear reigned over everything. In

administration, routine held sway; in the courts, formalism became scandalous. Life lay hidden in the minds and hearts of these young men, but it was sustained by them with some incomprehensible, firm hope that the present order could not continue for very long and that better days soon must come.[27]

Two factors or, more precisely, two individuals helped to stimulate the circle's interest in the French utopian socialists and applauded their more sharply focused criticisms of the Nicholas system in the late 1840s. One was Miliutin's younger brother Vladimir, and the other was Konstantin Kavelin, a well-known professor from Moscow University.

During his student years at the University of St. Petersburg, Vladimir Miliutin shared his brother's lodgings and brought to the Miliutin circle his interest in European political economy.[28] His essays on "The Proletariat and Pauperism in England and in France" and "Malthus and His Opponents," the first critique of Malthus's ideas in Russian, were known to the members of his brother's circle and may well have been discussed at its meetings. During the late 1840s, however, Vladimir Miliutin began to withdraw from their company to associate with the *Petrashevtsy* and with the esoteric, erotic salon that assembled at the home of G. N. Gennadi.[29] More sensitive and thoughtful than his elder brothers, Vladimir, like a number of other intellectuals during the late 1840s and early 1850s, was intellectually, even physically, destroyed by the "censorship terror" that pressed upon him. This was a time when erotic—sometimes simply pornographic—literature enjoyed a surge of popularity among those very men who not so long before had sworn to serve truth, love, and beauty. Ivan Turgenev, who lived in St. Petersburg during these years, attributed this directly to the manner in which these sensitive men reacted to Nicholas I's repressive regime. In discussing Boccaccio's *Decameron* and the manner in which elegant lords and ladies amused each other with obscene tales in order to forget about the terrible plagues that raged around them, he posed the question to his friends: "And really, wasn't the Nicholas oppression its own type of plague for educated society?"[30] Certainly Turgenev had a point. Men who had been (and would again become) some of Russia's most creative and sensitive writers abandoned their nightly debates about Russia's past, present, and future and devoted their evenings to pornographic verse, to whores, and to compulsive gambling and drinking.[31] For Vladimir Miliutin, these years had fatal consequences; most probably at Gennadi's, he contracted syphilis and died before the age of thirty.[32]

More pragmatic, more realistic, and more hopeful, those in Miliutin's circle did not follow the path of his younger brother, and the urgings of Konstantin Kavelin helped to direct their discussions about change toward workable alternatives. As the ominous clouds of political reaction settled over Russia, Kavelin and his close friend on the Moscow University faculty, Petr Redkin, abandoned their professorial chairs to seek refuge in the St. Petersburg bureaucracy. Both took posts in Miliutin's Municipal Section, and Kavelin edited a number of the important new statistical studies that were being compiled in Miliutin's office.[33]

A deeply committed Hegelian, a strong opponent of serfdom, and a thinker well-acquainted with the works of the French utopian socialists, Kavelin soon became the Miliutin circle's mentor, much as he had served as preceptor for students at Moscow University earlier in the decade. Yet the political repression that drove him from his chair at the university did not cause him to reject his belief in the renovating power of autocracy. "I believe completely in the necessity of absolutism in present-day Russia, but it ought to be progressive and enlightened," he wrote to his friend Granovskii soon after he reached the capital.[34]

Because Miliutin's circle believed in orderly, evolutionary change, the publicist Pavel Annenkov dubbed it the "Petersburg Party of Progress."[35] By the late 1840s, their ranks included not only the men we have mentioned, but also Aleksandr Girs (one of Miliutin's closest associates in the Municipal Section), Konstantin Grot (who became Governor of Samara in 1853), Evgenii Korsh (a leading Westerner and friend of Herzen), the young Westerner historian Boris Chicherin (during his visits to St. Petersburg), Petr Redkin, Iakov and Nikolai Khanykov (both *litseisty*, whose brother Aleksandr was an ardent disciple of Fourier and one of Chernyshevskii's intellectual mentors in the late 1840s), V. S. Poroshin (regarded by many as the most exciting professor at St. Petersburg University), and Andrei Kraevskii, editor of *Otechestvennye zapiski*.[36] Together, these men used the Ministries of Internal Affairs and State Domains to improve their knowledge about Russia, and they even seized control of the Russian Geographical Society in order to direct its resources toward the same end. As mid-century approached, they extended their associations, and, by the outbreak of the Crimean War, they had established ties with almost every progressive group in the capital. At the same time, through the efforts of Kavelin, Korsh, and Chicherin, they cemented relations with circles in Moscow and with such leading intellectuals as Granovskii and Mikhail Pogodin.[37] Perhaps most important of all, the Miliutin circle bridged the chasms that had opened between various groups of the intelligentsia earlier in the 1840s. Although in many ways sympathetic to the views of the Westerners in the great debate that tore the ranks of the intelligentsia apart, they also preserved close ties with Slavophiles and proponents of Official Nationality.

Miliutin and his closest friends achieved this seemingly impossible reconciliation of bitter opposites by offering an opportunity to engage in "practical" work within the government to those men whose views had denied them any political role. As a result of these efforts, not only the Westerners Kavelin and Redkin but also the Slavophiles Ivan Aksakov and Iurii Samarin held positions in the Economic Department of the Ministry of Internal Affairs. Here they found it possible to work together productively and effectively despite the acrimonious debates that continued to divide their friends during the last decade of the Nicholas era. In the Economic Department this reconciliation was achieved only on a limited scale, but the effectiveness of meaningful political action as a means of reconciliation soon was proved far more conclusively in the legislative preparations for the Great Reforms themselves. Those Westerners and Slavophiles who participated in the discussions of various government committees hastened to bury their differences and reconciled themselves with each other and with the state. Only among those who were excluded from the reform preparations did the debate of the 1840s continue.

One of the first circles with which Miliutin and his friends became acquainted in St. Petersburg was that of Nikolai Nedezhdin and Konstantin Nevolin. Especially for those among them who had not studied at the university, this broadened their views, for Nadezhdin and Nevolin counted some of Russia's leading scholars among their friends. Born the son of a parish priest in 1804, Nadezhdin had studied at the Moscow Ecclesiastical Academy and then at Moscow University.[38] He soon became a disciple of Kant and Schelling and, after finishing his doctoral dissertation in 1831, received a post at Moscow University. Belinskii, Nikolai Stankevich, and Konstantin Aksakov heard his lectures and were moved by them to devote themselves to the study of Schelling's ideas. During these years, Nadezhdin became a close friend of former Minister of Justice Ivan Dmitriev and of Mikhail Pogodin. A number of aristocratic literary critics resented his sharply worded reviews of Pushkin's work and called Nadezhdin's writing "very common and vulgar."[39] Nonetheless, his career bore every promise of success until he became the editor of *Teleskop*, a journal in which many of the younger generation of Moscow literary community participated. Konstantin Aksakov, Mikhail Zagoskin, the poet Iazykov, Belinskii, Herzen, Ivan Kireevskii, Ivan Panaev, and a number of others all contributed to its pages, and despite opposition from the Moscow "establishment" (including most importantly the powerful Nikolai Grech), *Teleskop* flourished until Nadezhdin published Chaadaev's first "Philosophical letter." Success changed quickly into persecution as the authorities declared Chaadaev insane and sent Nadezhdin to Ust'-Sysol'sk. Thanks to several powerful friends, among them Iakov Rostovtsev, he was freed from Siberian exile after several years and went to live in the Crimea.[40]

Intercession by Perovskii made it possible for Nadezhdin to enter government service in St. Petersburg as editor of *The Journal of the Ministry of Internal Affairs*. As a number of his Moscow friends moved to St. Petersburg, he again became involved with scholarly and literary circles and soon renewed his friendship with Belinskii and Panaev. Most of all, he enjoyed the company of Konstantin Nevolin, also a priest's son, who became perhaps their closest friend during their years in the capital.[41] As one of the three best students at the Moscow Ecclesiastical Academy, Nevolin had been assigned to work on codification in the Second Section, and Speranskii then had sent him to study law at the universities of Berlin, Göttingen, and Heidelberg.[42] He returned to St. Petersburg to receive a doctorate in civil law and then taught for several years at Kiev's University of St. Vladimir. In 1843, the year that Nadezhdin became editor of *The Journal of the Ministry of Internal Affairs*, Nevolin was appointed Professor of Russian Civil Law at St. Petersburg University.[43] Widely regarded as Russia's preeminent authority on civil law during the 1840s, Nevolin shared with Nadezhdin an apartment where a number of prominent academics gathered. Among them were V. V. Grigor'ev, P. S. Savel'ev, I. P. Sakharov, V. V. Skripitsyn, and Vladimir Dal'.[44]

Dal', a close friend of Nevolin and Nadezhdin and already widely acclaimed as an ethnographer and lexicographer, had been the first of Russia's literary figures whom Perovskii brought into the Ministry of Internal Affairs. He had earned a doctorate in medicine at the University of Dorpat, had participated in the famous Khiva expedition led by Pervoskii's younger brother in 1839–1840, and, during most of Perovskii's tenure, directed his personal chancery.[45] Like Nadezhdin, Dal' was a specialist on Russian sectarians and later published several studies about the *khlysty* and the *skoptsy* based on materials he had obtained with Perovskii's help.[46] Perovskii considered Dal' one of his most valuable aides and placed an extraordinary amount of confidence in his judgment.[47]

Like Dal' and Nadezhdin, V. V. Grigor'ev, an orientalist who had studied at St. Petersburg and Moscow Universities between 1831 and 1842, was one of Perovskii's recruits[48] and served as Nadezhdin's assistant until 1851, when he transferred to the provincial capital of Orenburg to be closer to the region upon which his scholarly work had come to focus.[49] His interests in eastern studies were shared in the Nevolin-Nadezhdin circle by his friend P. S. Savel'ev, the son of a Petersburg merchant and also educated at the University of St. Petersburg. Savel'ev was a numismatist, especially interested in Central Asia, and became the secretary of the Committee on Foreign Censorship (1841–1852), where he had access to the latest works published in the West.[50]

The remaining two leading figures in the Nadezhdin-Nevolin circle shared Nadezhdin's interests in Slavic culture and religion. Ivan Petrovich Sakharov, like Nevolin and Nadezhdin the son of a priest, had studied medicine at Moscow University and had come to St. Petersburg in 1836 to serve in the Postal Department. Beginning in the 1830s, and continuing until illness made it impossible for him to continue his work in the mid-1850s, Sakharov published a large scholarly corpus about peasant life. His work added a rare dimension to the experience of friends who were less acquainted with the world outside the community of scholars than he was.[51] Sakharov was deeply patriotic, as were Nadezhdin and V. V. Skripitsyn, the other leading member of the group. Unlike the rest of the Nevolin-Nadezhdin circle, Skripitsyn was a nobleman who had begun his career in the Imperial Guards. As was common in the Nicholaean service, he had exchanged his Guards' epaulettes for the uniform of a civil servant and, by the 1840s, had become director of the Department of Ecclesiastical Affairs of Foreign Faiths in Perovskii's ministry. Skripitsyn, the least scholarly of the group, was known for his russification policies in his dealings with foreign faiths within the Empire.[52]

The Nadezhdin-Nevolin circle was thus unusual in St. Petersburg's intellectual and service milieux because all but one of its early members were of non-noble origin. That single factor may have helped them to bridge the gap between the intelligentsia and the bureaucracy in the mid-1840s. Mavericks in both worlds, they tended not to be bound by the constraints that governed either. Due to the diversity of its membership and its unique connection with the Petersburg worlds of scholarship, intelligentsia, and government service, the Nadezhdin-Nevolin circle served Miliutin, Zablotskii, and some of their closest friends as a means for establishing closer contacts with the intelligentsia and St. Petersburg's scholarly community during the mid-1840s.[53] It also acquainted them with other young officials who shared their views—most notably Aleksandr Golovnin and Iurii Samarin—whom Dal' often brought as his guests to these evening gatherings and who soon became a part of their group.[54]

Contact between the intelligentsia and St. Petersburg's progressive young bureaucrats was facilitated during the 1840s and early 1850s because, as we mentioned earlier, increasing numbers of the intelligentsia entered the bureaucracy in order to withdraw from public view at that time. We already have discussed how this affected the Ministries of Internal Affairs and State Domains, but it also extended to other agencies. The critic and writer A. V. Druzhinin, the young satirist Mikhail Saltykov, the playwright V. R. Zotov, and V. A. Tsie (who later played an important part in discussions about local government reform), served as civilian officials in the War Ministry during the 1840s. Saltykov, Zotov, and Tsie all were *litseisty*, and that bond drew them together in the ministry's offices.[55] Likewise, the writer and editor Panaev, the critic, censor, and editor A. V. Nikitenko, and the novelist Goncharov all served with Nadezhdin's friend Savel'ev, while the *litseisty* Evgenii Lamanskii and Mikhail Reitern served in the Ministry of Finance.

It would be impossible to reconstruct all the interconnecting relationships that tied these men into a loosely knit group, unified in what Prince Obolenskii called "the desire for a better order."[56] Yet the fragmentary sources indicate that there was considerable contact between progressive young officials and the St. Petersburg intelligentsia outside the bureaucracy as well. During the early 1850s, gatherings dominated by such literary figures as Ostrovskii, Pisemskii, and Grigorovich met every Thursday at Kraevskii's lodgings. These also were frequented by Nikolai and Dmitrii Miliutin, Zablotskii, and other "important officials,"[57] according to the scholar and literary critic A. N. Pypin. Zablotskii even reportedly served as the model for one of Goncharov's characters in *Obyknovennaia istoriia*.[58] Other groups met at the lodgings of Prince Odoevskii, who served so ably as Zablotskii's co-editor of *Sel'skoe chtenie*, and at the Zhemchuzhnikovs', where a number of *pravovedy*, including V. A. Artsimovich and Prince Obolenskii, gathered during the late 1840s.[59]

Miliutin, Zablotskii, and their close associates most frequently met the St. Petersburg intelligentsia at the evening gatherings which Ivan Panaev held every week. Panaev had been educated at the Boarding School for Sons of the Nobility at St. Petersburg University, entered the bureaucracy in 1831, and, beginning in 1834, served in the Ministry of Public Instruction. An affluent aristocrat, he moved easily in St. Petersburg's high society and was well acquainted with a number of prominent statesmen, including Minister of Finance Kankrin.[60] He followed the intellectual path of Russia's romantic youth of the 1830s. Like them, he saw "society in eternal struggle with the poet" and concluded that the two were separated by an unbridgeable chasm. "Society will never rise to the poet's level," he once wrote, "and the poet will never descend to the level of society."[61]

Soon after Panaev met Belinskii in 1839, he embarked upon that reconciliation with reality that characterized the intellectual odysseys of Herzen, Belinskii, and others. Herzen's preachings during 1840 convinced Belinskii that reality must be challenged and that the human personality could have meaning only in a struggle against the oppressions of the external world.[62] Following that path, Panaev, too, concluded that the artist must be the conscience of his time and society. Along with Belinskii and Herzen, he had concluded that the artist, as the only effective agent to combat an immoral world, must work to alter society. Panaev expressed his commitment to this view through his active participation in Kraevskii's *Otechestvennye zapiski,* a new journal for which Belinskii served as chief literary critic and which, between 1840 and 1847, published important works by Herzen, Nekrasov, Ogarev, Saltykov, Granovskii, Dostoevskii, Vladimir Miliutin, Zablotskii, and many others.[63] Until Panaev and Nekrasov assumed the editorship of *Sovremennik* in 1846, and took Belinskii, Turgenev, Goncharov, and a number of other leading *intelligenty* with them, *Otechestvennye zapiski* was the leading forum for progressive opinion in Russia.

Panaev's close connection with *Otechestvennye zapiski* made him a central figure in a literary circle that met at his lodgings throughout the 1840s and early 1850s. Its most prominent early members included Belinskii, Nekrasov, Turgenev, Botkin, Kraevskii, Herzen, Ogarev, Count Sollogub, Dal', Kavelin, and Grigorovich.[64] During the early 1840s, Belinskii's passion for the French Revolution became a major preoccupation during many of their evenings as they studied and read together. "Although they did not know French," Panaev later recalled, "Belinskii and many of our friends . . . gathered at my lodgings each Saturday and I read to them what I had managed to compile and translate [from *Histoire parlementaire de la révolution française*] in the course of the previous week."[65] During these years, Panaev also translated "whole notebooks of Lamartine, Louis Blanc, and others" for his guests,[66] and not long afterwards, works by Proudhon, Cabet, and Fourier became objects of his circle's enthusiasm.[67]

Zablotskii, Miliutin, and their close friends were not part of Panaev's gatherings during the early 1840s, but they began to appear there during the middle of the decade, as a result of their growing friendship with Kraevskii.[68] During the late 1840s, their associations broadened further as a result of Vladimir Miliutin's close connection with the *Sovremennik* circle and Kavelin's long-standing friendship with Belinskii. Kavelin had known Belinskii ever since 1834, when his parents had hired the young critic as a tutor for their son.[69] During the eleven months he spent in St. Petersburg during 1842, Kavelin had been closely associated with Panaev's circle, and, when he returned to serve in Miliutin's Municipal Section in 1848, he hastened to renew his friendship with his former comrades. In doing so he brought the progressive officials with whom he served into a much more meaningful relationship with Panaev. By mid-century, Ivan Arapetov, Zablotskii, Miliutin, and Prince Obolenskii all became regular visitors at his evening gatherings.[70] No longer were they bureaucrats who stood apart from the society and the debates of the intelligentsia. They had become respected figures in both milieux.

The Imperial Russian Geographical Society

St. Petersburg's progressive young officials carried the exchange of views that they had begun with the circles of Nadezhdin, Nevolin, and Panaev into the more sedate confines of the Imperial Russian Geographical Society during the late 1840s and early 1850s. Between 1845 and 1856, 513 men from St. Petersburg's bureaucratic, literary, and scholarly communities became full members of this organization, in addition to thirty-nine others who were associate members.[71] In the Russian Geographical Society, "modestly housed on the third floor of Utin's residence on the Moika," as one member recalled,[72] these men broadened their ideas about reform and made serious efforts to assemble accurate demographic data and material about social and economic conditions in Russia's countryside. Most important, they tried to make their new knowledge available to more educated Russians. So popular did the society become among educated young men in mid-nineteenth-century Russia that Baron M. A. Korf, a close confidant of the Emperor, feared that it might one day threaten the autocrat's power. The Society, he remarked, "by its unusual collection of young men [who gather] for conversation on subjects about public affairs presents something not easily tolerated in an enlightened autocracy."[73] Contrary to Korf's fears, the Geographical Society actually became an instrument for the defense of enlightened autocracy in Russia. During the last decade of the Nicholas era, when reaction ruled the Empire and oppression lay heavily upon men who favored reform or renovation, it offered an alternative between complete rejection of the State's policies and total acquiescence. It provided men who supported the precepts of autocracy but believed with Kavelin that they "ought to be progressive and enlightened,"[74] with an opportunity to follow a middle path, to broaden their studies of Russian conditions and thereby nourish their hope for a better future.

Much has been written about the oppression that Russian intellectuals suffered during the Nicholas era, and we need not summarize it here. But to portray the second quarter of the nineteenth century as a time of unmitigated oppression and political obscurantism is to repeat only that side of the story told so dramatically by such alienated intellectuals as Herzen, Belinskii, and Panaev, who suffered from tyrannical censors' pens. Without doubt, Nicholas's reign encompassed what the scholar

Mikhail Lemke once called the "epoch of censorship terror," but it also was the Golden Age of Russian Literature. It saw some of Russia's first great composers and painters emerge, and it marked the development of Russian theater to a point where it assumed an identity of its own. Jurists began to be trained in Russia during these years, and the youths educated at the School of Jurisprudence later provided the expertise for making the Judicial Reform Statutes of 1864 perhaps the most successful of the Great Reforms. That so much intellectual and scholarly endeavor flourished during the Nicholas era is evidence that many educated Russians reconciled themselves to its constraints and found it possible to work creatively and successfully within such limits.

Nowhere was the Nicholas system more lavish in support of learning than in the field of applied science, which Uvarov, creator of the trilological doctrine of "Orthodoxy, Autocracy, and Nationality," sought to develop for the welfare of Russians and the glory of their rulers. As its new charter, drafted under Uvarov's supervision, read, the Academy of Sciences "must keep the government posted on all discoveries made by its members or foreign scholars that will abet the safeguarding of public health or lead to improvements in industry, the arts, manufacturing, trade, and shipping."[75] Uvarov also labored to make the Academy of Sciences in St. Petersburg a "showcase of Russia's contribution to modern scientific thought,"[76] and he extended this view into other parts of the scientific establishment. With steadfast dedication, he recruited noted scientists, first from the University of Dorpat, and then from universities throughout Europe.

Uvarov's efforts produced spectacular results. He brought to St. Petersburg, Karl Ernst von Baer, who began his career as an embryologist but broadened the range of his scientific enquiry immensely once he settled in St. Petersburg. In the tradition of Alexander von Humboldt, whom Nicholas personally had invited to explore the Ural, Caspian, and Altai regions of the Empire in 1829, von Baer pioneered a scientific study of the Empire's natural resources based on the work of specialists.[77] In addition to von Baer, Uvarov recruited others: Hermann Heinrich Hess, the founder of thermochemistry; Heinrich F. E. Lenz, the discoverer of Lenz's law on the direction of induced electrical current; Moritz Jacobi, a pioneer in galvanoplastics; the physicist A. T. Kupffer; and the zoologists Alexander Middendorff and Johann Brandt.[78] Such support for applied science led to the establishment of the world-renowned observatory at Pulkovo directed by the great astronomer Friedrich Georg Wilhelm von Struve, who fostered the measurement of the Russo-Scandinavian arc, "one of the greatest scientific undertakings of nineteenth-century Russia."[79]

The Geographical Society provided an important example of Nicholas's support for scientific endeavor. Its founding was the result of urgings by explorers[80] and academicians[81] seeking to pursue scientific interests, energetic Imperial General Staff officers who urged further geographical study of areas into which the Empire was seeking to expand,[82] and a few progressive government officials who realized that more research about Russia's demography and agriculture could be useful in developing better policies.[83] Encouraged by their enthusiasm, Nicholas approved plans to establish the Geographical Society on August 6, 1845. Its temporary charter was modeled on that of Britain's Royal Geographical Society, with the provision that within four years its members would draft a permanent one. Called the Imperial Russian Geographical Society, it was financed by an annual grant of 10,000 rubles from the Imperial Treasury, and Grand Duke Konstantin Nikolaevich, Nicholas's second son, became its first president.[84]

As with the Academy of Sciences, non-Russians dominated the Geographical Society from the beginning and, of its fifty-one founders, the names of thirty-one bespoke foreign or Baltic German origin. Baron Vrangel directed its Section on General Geography; von Struve, that on the Geography of Russia; von Baer headed the Section on Ethnography; and Keppen presided over the Section on Statistics. F. P. Litke, a Baltic German naval officer who was tutor and companion to Grand Duke Konstantin Nikolaevich, became its vice-president. All were part of the Uvarovian scientific establishment in the Academy of Sciences; all were devoted to the Uvarovian principle that applied science should be employed to win international acclaim for Russia; all saw themselves as a part of Russia's social and scientific elite. Undoubtedly, most of them hoped to see the Society rival its British model, just as the Pulkovo Observatory already had begun to rival that at Greenwich.

The Geographical Society was begun as an arm of the Uvarovian scientific establishment designed to pursue science for the greater glory of Russia, although some of its founders disliked Uvarov personally and chafed at the slowness with which he made decisions.[85] Among its founders, only Zablotskii, Dal', Nadezhdin, Arsen'ev, and Prince Odoevskii represented the views of St. Petersburg's progressive young officials.[86] Probably none of its founders, including even Zablotskii, expected that within half a decade the Society would become a major instrument for advancing economic, demographic, and social studies of those regions destined to be touched most directly by the Great Reforms.

The efforts of Aleksandr Golovnin, chosen at the age of twenty-four to serve as the Society's secretary, were particularly important in enabling progressive officials to gain such influence in its affairs.[87] Born into a famous noble family on March 25, 1821, Golovnin was a sickly child who sought refuge in books from a household dominated by women.[88] During his early adolescent years, he immersed himself in the works of Derzhavin, Lomonosov, Kheraskov, Sumarokov, Fonvizin, Batiushkov, and Bariatinskii. He read and re-read Karamzin's *History of the Russian State,* and from it developed a love for Russia, a sense of her potential greatness, and a belief in autocracy.[89] His formal education began as a day student on a state scholarship at the First Petersburg Gymnasium. Accustomed only to the company of his mother and sisters, he suffered cruelly from the taunts of his schoolmates, until his mother was able to enroll him at the Lyceum at Tsarskoe Selo in 1835.[90] There Golovnin found the company of youths committed to the Lyceum's tradition of close comradeship deeply gratifying, for it was not uncommon for adolescent youths to find physical as well as intellectual satisfaction among their comrades at the Empire's elite schools.[91] In this more congenial atmosphere, Golovnin continued to devour the writings of Byron, Goethe, Schiller, Pushkin, and Zhukovskii, and he thus became imbued with the same intellectual and emotional outlook that Miliutin, Zablotskii, Zarudnyi, and others like them carried away from school to their first chancery assignments.[92]

Golovnin at first found it difficult to reconcile his dreams with life in St. Petersburg's chanceries. He had won the Lyceum's gold medal, given only to those who ranked first in their class, and had entered the civil service at the comparatively high rank of *tituliarnyi sovetnik* (grade nine). He first served in the Fourth Section of His Majesty's Own Chancery under N. M. Longinov, a close friend of his deceased father, whom he described as "an honorable and kindly old gentleman."[93] For Golovnin, however, the work was intellectually deadening. As he later described these months (his memoirs are written entirely in the third person), "his service duties were not tiring, but they were devoid of meaning, involving first correspondence and then the task of preparing documents about the administration of girls' schools."[94] When Golovnin transferred to Dal's office in the Ministry of Internal Affairs, he found his place in the service. Dal' assigned him work he considered useful, and he devoted long hours to his new responsibilities. Golovnin found in Dal' a mentor to be respected and admired,[95] much as Miliutin and Zablotskii had found such models in Perovskii and Kiselev. Yet Golovnin's relationship with his superior differed markedly from theirs. Dal' stood only three grades above his protégé in the Table of Ranks, frequently invited him to meetings of the Nadezhdin-Nevolin circle, and introduced him to Nikolai and Dmitrii Miliutin, the Khanykov brothers, and Iurii Samarin.[96]

Dal's confidence in Golovnin's intellectual and administrative talents, and the respect that such explorers as Litke had for his father's memory, led to his appointment as secretary of the Geographical Society in October 1845.[97] Since it was the responsibility of the Society's secretary to serve as the president's assistant, Litke may have supported Golovnin in the hope that he could bridge the gap that separated Grand Duke Konstantin Nikolaevich, who held no official service rank at the time, from St. Petersburg's official world.[98] Perhaps more important, he may have seen Golovnin, so highly recommended by his fellow Baltic German Dal', as someone who would defend the interests of Russia's foreign scholarly establishment within the Society. If that were his purpose, Golovnin at first more than fulfilled his expectations. "News of the Geographical Society interests me greatly. Our meticulous secretary sends me whole notebooks about it and I am extremely grateful to him," he wrote to Baron Vrangel that November.[99]

During the last half of the 1840s, Golovnin worked to bring progressive officials into the Geographical Society. His reasons for doing so are not clear, and he passes over this important question in his memoirs. Certainly, patriotic feelings and the desire of young educated Russians to break the grip of German scholars upon their scientific establishment may have been one reason, and it is one that has received ample attention in the few accounts that have been written about the Geographical Society during the past century.[100] But what historians have so frequently portrayed simply as a nationalistic Russian effort to overcome German dominance in their scientific establishment was, in fact, considerably more complex. Faced by policies of retrenchment that made it difficult for them to continue their studies of Russian conditions after 1848, progressive young officials tried to seize the Society because it was the institution outside the bureaucracy best able to support their work.

One cannot say for certain that this latter purpose was foremost in Golovnin's mind when be began to bring friends from the bureaucracy into the Geographical Society in 1846, but what may have begun as an attempt to increase Russian influence turned into a concerted effort by progressive officials to seize control. Of the 170 new members added to the Society during the next two years, the names of only thirty-nine readily identify them as being of probable foreign or Baltic German origin. Most important, seventeen of Golovnin's new recruits were prominent among those who emerged as the core of Russia's enlightened bureaucracy or were closely allied with them.[101] During the eighteen months after the revolutions of 1848 in Europe, seven more progressive young officials were recruited,[102] and, by 1850, at least thirty were members. That twenty-two of them were in the Section on Russian Statistics offers further evidence for their purpose in joining.

These were talented, energetic men, by that time well schooled in the arena of bureaucratic and academic intrigue. When confronted by their challenge, the middle-aged "German" scholars, undisputed for so long in the preeminent positions which Russia's scholarly and scientific establishment had bestowed upon them, could not parry their attack. Further, when these young men began an offensive in late 1849, Uvarov had been replaced in office by the unassertive Prince Shirinskii-Shikhmatov, who admitted to "neither thought nor will of my own. I am only the blind tool of the Sovereign's will," he proclaimed with misguided pride.[103] When the so-called "German party" in the Society was challenged, the Emperor did not make his will known. Shirinskii-Shikhmatov thus did nothing to defend the influence of the scientific elite which Uvarov had assembled in St. Petersburg and nurtured with such care.

Signs of the coming conflict were evident in April 1846, when Litke wrote at length to Baron Vrangel about the first skirmishes between a few progressive young officials and Russia's scientific establishment:

> What they tell me about the [Geographical Society] meeting of April 9th, I do not like overly much, and if the spirit or, perhaps more precisely, the habit of argument, takes root in the form in which it came to light in that meeting, then the development [of the Society] in a scholarly direction will be completely repressed and factionalism will develop in its place. . . . It is essential that all right-thinking members close ranks around the president and support him. At the April meeting there was no one—or almost no one —of those upon whom he could rely and lean: not you, nor Baer, nor Struve. It would be sinful and sad if our infant (as we call the Geographical Society) at its very birth should suffocate in the fumes of discord.[104]

Although writing to Vrangel about marshaling support for Konstantin Nikolaevich as president, Litke was in fact speaking of mobilizing the senior scholarly and scientific community for its own defense. The conflict remained muted for some eighteen months but broke out sharply when it came time to draw up the Society's permanent charter. Late in 1847, a drafting committee of eight was chosen to work under Litke's direction. Von Baer, Gelmersen, Fuss, and E. K. Meiendorff defended the views of the scholarly establishment, while Nikolai and Dmitrii Miliutin, supported by Poroshin, opposed them.[105] The eighth member, P. N. Musin-Pushkin, stood between the two factions.

Litke and his supporters urged that the Society continue to emulate the Royal Geographical Society, in order to keep most of the decision-making power in the hands of a Council they controlled. Poroshin and the Miliutins insisted that the Council be subordinated to the Society's General Assembly[106] and, as one scholar wrote recently, stood "for the full democratization of the Society."[107] What they advocated, according to Dmitrii Miliutin, was to "extend participation in scholarly activity to a broader circle of members"[108] and, as his brother Nikolai commented further, to make certain that "scholarly questions and proposals concerning the entire Society are decided in its General Assembly [and not in its Council]."[109] What they hoped to achieve, in the view of one observer, was to redirect the Society toward statistical and ethnographic research about European Russia, while the scholarly establishment, in the tradition of such German mentors and colleagues as von Humboldt and Ritter, wanted to employ its resources for exploring uncharted regions of the Empire.[110]

The challengers of the scholarly establishment had not yet gained the power base needed to win control, for Litke had the ear of Konstantin Nikalaevich, and, with his support, the views of the establishment prevailed.[111] St. Petersburg's young progressives did not abandon their struggle but adopted new tactics. Their small, well-planned guerrilla foray to capture the Society's ramparts had shown them a breach in the walls themselves and, in 1849, they found the means to lauch a mass assault that the scholarly establishment could not repel. The Miliutins, Zablotskii, Poroshin, and their friends argued that the Society should be "Russian" in its composition and interests, a point which Nikolai Miliutin had emphasized in April 1847[112] and which Iakov Khanykov had repeated in his arguments for geographical terminology based on Russian rather than foreign words.[113] At a time when the number of Russians in the Society was increasing, but when the vice-president and all four heads of its Sections were of Baltic German or foreign origin, these calls for the Society to become "Russian" struck a sympathetic chord. Continuing to sow these fertile seeds of discontent, the young progressive officials reaped their harvest early the following year.

On February 16, 1850, the Geographical Society held its first elections under a permanent charter, and the progressive bureaucrats' campaign for "Russianness" yielded surprising results. Litke was ousted from his post and replaced as the Society's vice-president by General M. N. Murav'ev, a man of reactionary views and little geographical expertise but one known for being "Russian" in his outlook. Murav'ev's victory was symbolically important, but the election of the Society's Council members and the heads of its four Sections was of more consequence for controlling its direction and resources. "Germans" representing the scholarly establishment were replaced by "Russians." Only von Struve kept his post, while Baron Vrangel, Keppen, and von Baer were replaced by A. D. Ozerskii, Zablotskii, and Nadezhdin. In addition, the Council included F. F. Berg, A. M. Kniazhevich, A. I. Levshin, Baron E. K. Meiendorff, Dmitrii Miliutin, A. S. Norov, P. A. Tuchkov, and I. P.

Shul'gin. The Society's new secretary was A. K. Girs, a close friend of Zablotskii and the Miliutins.

From their position of dominance on the Society's Council, St. Petersburg's enlightened bureaucrats consolidated their control over its resources. At least eleven of the seventeen members of the editorial board of *Geograficheskie izvestiia*—the Society's monthly publication and most important organ for directing its research—were from their ranks or sympathetic to their goal of supporting ethnographic and statistical studies of Russia,[114] and Kraevskii, their friend and associate since the mid-1840s, became its editor. This new editorial board changed the name of their journal, as a signal to the Society's members that they were fulfilling their pledge to make the Geographical Society more "Russian," and *Geograficheskie izvestiia* became *Vestnik Imperatorskago Russkago Geograficheskago Obshchestva* in 1851. To strengthen their control over the Society they recruited more men who they were confident would support their aims. Of 118 new members taken into the Geographical Society between 1851 and 1856, sixty were nominated by eleven progressive officials who drafted the Great Reforms or were very closely associated with those who did.[115] During precisely those years when it was most difficult to pursue studies of provincial social and economic conditions within the regular agencies of the central bureaucracy these men dominated the Society, and then, in 1857, when it became possible to resume their work within the regular bureaucracy, they abandoned it to St. Petersburg's scholarly establishment.[116] In the 1857 elections, Litke was elected vice-president almost unanimously, while von Baer and Gelmersen returned to the Society's Council. Although Russia's enlightened bureaucrats continued to be members after that, the years of their most energetic participation were over.

While they controlled the Geographical Society, the enlightened bureaucrats used it to carry out statistical and ethnographic studies that further prepared them for the role they would play in drafting the Great Reforms. To them, the problems Russia faced at mid-century no longer could be stated in terms of administrative bureaus that functioned ineffectively or of officials who fulfilled their duties imperfectly or improperly. By the late 1840s, they had become convinced that the arbitrary power of nobles and officials must be curbed, that serfdom eventually must be abolished, that the judicial system must be reformed, and that the lives of everyone in Russia must be ruled by law. They must harness the forces of social change and create a broader base of support for autocracy that somehow allowed Russians some amount of participation in their government.

To carry out these complex tasks they faced many difficulties, not the least of which was the need to obtain accurate information about

Russia's population. Even mid-nineteenth-century censuses could be considered only reasonably accurate calculations of males from the tax-paying classes of the Empire because very sizable and significant portions of the population, including women, nobles, and government officials were not regularly inscribed.[117] When Zablotskii and his friends seized control of the Geographical Society, government statisticians were about to begin the ninth official census. They hoped to use their new positions in the Society to implement census procedures that would provide such data about religion, age, nationality, occupation, and family size as modern statisticians and statesmen considered vital to informed policy-making. But control of the census was in the hands of Minister of Finance F. P. Vronchenko, a traditionalist whose reluctance to argue for innovations in the conservative Nicholaean financial establishment had helped his rise to ministerial rank.[118] Because of Vronchenko's opposition, Zablotskii and his supporters in the Society's Statistical Section had to give way. Late in 1856, they tried again, this time with the support of Keppen who, with the backing of the Society's entire Council, urged Konstantin Nikolaevich to support conducting the 1857 census according to more scientific principles.[119] This time the new Minister of Finance P. F. Brok proved just as adamant in opposing change. Even in combination with other scholarly and scientific institutions, Petr Semenov, one of nineteenth-century Russia's greatest statisticians, concluded that it would be impossible for the Geographical Society to attain its goals "so long as the government does not take legislative measures for producing a general and accurate census of the population of the entire Empire."[120] The tsarist government did not heed Semenov's repeated pleas until 1897.

Unsuccessful in compiling more comprehensive information about Russia's population, Zablotskii and his associates in the Geographical Society's Statistical Section turned to less ambitious and controversial undertakings. Data in government files remained too limited to study economic or social problems on an Empire-wide basis. Therefore, they continued those local and regional studies for which they could assemble the necessary data through first-hand observation. Their most successful effort was Ivan Aksakov's study of the eleven commercial fairs in the Ukraine. His study, published in 1858, provided valuable information about Russian internal trade and manufacture that had never been available to the government before and earned the prestigious Konstantinovskii medal for its author. The enlightened bureaucrats also were more successful in their ethnographic researches. Of particular importance was the success of the Society's periodical publication, *Etnograficheskii sbornik,* edited first by Nadezhdin and then by Kavelin, who urged the Ethnographical Section of the Society to pursue provincial, not Empire-wide, studies and to place them in a broader historical context.[121]

Although control of the Geographical Society did not yield all they had hoped for between 1850 and 1857, it provided Russia's enlightened bureaucrats with important opportunities to investigate internal trade, population movements, and local life in the Empire and to transmit their findings to a wider audience.[122] Equally important, it brought together men who had not yet become acquainted in the course of their government assignments. Iu. A. Gagemeister, a graduate of Dorpat University, and E. I. Lamanskii, a *litseist,* both of whom had spent their early careers in the conservative Ministry of Finance, established those common links with Miliutin, Zablotskii, Arapetov, and Girs in the Statistical Section of the Geographical Society, which cemented the alliance they carried into the Editing Commissions of 1859–1860.[123] The same was true of S. M. Zhukovskii, who served on the Editing Commissions, and of Ia. A. Solov'ev, a young official in the Ministry of State Domains who rose to become an important figure in the enlightened bureaucrats' ranks by the mid-1850s. Like Miliutin, Solov'ev helped to prepare the *zemstvo* reforms of 1864 and draft the Emancipation of 1861.

With the exception of Prince V. A. Cherkasskii and the specialists who drafted the Judicial Reform of 1864, every government official who helped to draft and support the Great Reform legislation took an active part in the Geographical Society between 1850 and 1857. "Given the absence of any civic life among us at that time, the existence of such a center [as the Geographical Society] in which people interested in knowledge could gather for general discussions had special value in the eyes of society," recalled F. G. Terner, a young civil servant who was well acquainted with Zablotskii and Miliutin during the last years of the Nicholas era.[124] For exchanging ideas and furthering an understanding of Russia, the Geographical Society thus was of considerable importance in that assembly of forces within the bureaucracy that preceded the beginning of reform work after the end of the Crimean War.

Coupled with their belief that change was an evolutionary process, the work of these progressive, well-educated young officials during these years led them to contemplate a gradual transformation of rural Russia. Through their common labors and continued interaction with the intelligentsia they coalesced into an enlightened bureaucracy: a group of officials who envisioned change in broader terms than the administrative adjustments championed by Perovskii, Kiselev, and Panin, who shared the social conscience of the intelligentsia, and who believed that, as educated men with an ever-broadening understanding of Russian conditions, they could utilize their superior knowledge for the benefit of all Russians. The manner in which they studied Russia's provinces, their initial vision of rural Russia's transformation, and the manner in which they emerged as an enlightened bureaucracy are the subjects of the following chapter.

chapter 4

An Enlightened Bureaucracy Emerges

"All that we have done thus far is not yet ripened fruit but only good seed. It is not yet a task that is completed, but only a good beginning."

                 Konstantin Arsen'ev

The initial purpose of the studies that Miliutin and Zablotskii fostered during the 1840s was to develop data that could be used to understand provincial conditions and improve the central administration's ability to resolve regional and local problems by drafting more precise regulations. "Survey the existing failings and areas in which practice does not conform to the law in the civic and economic organization of towns and cities," Miliutin instructed his agents of special commisions in 1845. "Lay the groundwork for assembling complete administrative statistics about these areas of concern and . . . seek the means for a better organization of civic and economic affairs in these municipalities."[1] These tasks were very similar to those that Zarudnyi had set for himself within the Ministry of Justice at about the same time as he and his associates set out to find the faults (what he called "imperfections") in Russia's laws.[2]

Although important, statistics were only one of several instruments required to resolve the problems Russia faced, and, as mid-century approached, these men began to look beyond new regulations and more efficient administration to a gradual transformation of the Empire's social and economic life. "Even if they are absolutely accurate, numbers alone cannot provide a full understanding of any given issue," Konstantin Veselovskii admitted in 1847. "A qualitative evaluation of any problem," he added, "also is necessary."[3] Veselovskii's statement was an early expression of the enlightened bureaucrats' perception that no matter how precise or complete, mere information could not serve as an effective instrument for renovating Russia's stagnant social and economic systems. By mid-century they had begun to understand that such data never could be more than an instrument for refining and perpetuating policy. That realization compelled them to confront the most complex dilemma that modern Russian statesmen yet had been obliged to face. No longer was it a question of implementing and perpetuating policy; they had to find the means to change it.

Ever since Peter the Great had abolished the Boiar Council that advised Muscovite tsars, Russia's autocrats had made policy and relied on their chosen agents to execute their will. Peter's monopoly over the process of policy-making in domestic affairs was even more certain because his closest adjutants often were not part of the Empire's civil administration and worked outside that administration to carry out his commissions. Changes in policy thus came as a result of his own perceptions of Russia's needs or, much more rarely, as a consequence of influence exerted upon him by favorites who held his confidence.

Throughout the eighteenth century, Russia's autocrats made policy as circumstances warranted or as their perceptions of the Empire's needs changed. On those few occasions when they felt the need to consult a broader segment of opinion, they created *ad hoc* advisory bodies which ranged from such small groups of Imperial favorites as the Empress Anna Ivanovna's Supreme Privy Council, the Unofficial Committee of Alexander I, and Nicholas I's Committee of December 6th, to such larger bodies as Catherine II's Legislative Commission. None had a place in Russia's regular administrative structure. Their size, membership, and responsibilities were determined by the autocrat's whim, and they served strictly at the ruler's pleasure. Technical expertise or a broad knowledge of Russian affairs never was a prerequisite for membership in these groups. Far more important was loyalty to the autocrat. Individuals or interest groups in Russia thus first had to win the sovereign's favor, if they helped to bring about changes in policy. The only alternative was the eighteenth-century palace revolutions during which disgruntled aristocrats overthrew rulers whose policies were unpopular or seemed ill-advised.

So long as Russia's administration remained relatively unstructured, and the problems facing it reasonably uncomplex, such crude means for implementing and changing policy posed no insurmountable problems. As the Empire's bureaucracy increased in numbers, took on more complex functions, and had to face more complicated problems in the post-Napoleonic era, it became increasingly difficult to implement policy and even more awkward to change it. No sovereign could hope to understand the baffling problems that Russia faced during the second quarter of the nineteenth century. Nicholas I could not propose direct solutions as Peter the Great had done, because the resolution of these problems required more expertise than any single individual could possess. Nicholas I had grown up in a world without the technology that so rapidly entered the lives of men and women in the 1840s and 1850s. An autocrat who had grown up in a world without railroads, steamships, or factories with steam-driven machinery could not easily change state policy to encompass the complex social and political problems that such technology created.

If the Emperor could not confront the problems facing his Empire in the direct manner of the eighteenth-century autocrats, the issue of changing policy was complicated further because the interests of the state and its nobles no longer coincided. Since most statesmen and senior officials still came from aristocratic, serf-owning families, they slowed the implementation of policies that stood against the traditional interests of their class.[4] Furthermore, the so-called "palace revolutions" that eighteenth-century Russian aristocrats had used to change policy no longer were effective in the post-Napoleonic era. There were a number of reasons for that, not the least of which was Paul I's Statute on the Imperial Family. Issued on the day of Paul's coronation, this decree established a firm order of succession and ended the unstable situation that the Empire's nobles had used to extort extensive privileges from eighteenth-century autocrats. The result was a stalemate in which the autocrat found it difficult to implement policies that were against the interests of the aristocracy, while the aristocracy found it even more difficult to force changes in those state policies they opposed.

This situation was complicated further because Russia's growing army of petty clerks, who had learned their narrow duties on the job, opposed any change for fear that such might burden them with new tasks that they might be unable to learn.[5] These thousands of poorly educated, underpaid men, whose lives we described briefly in the first chapter of this study, stood as a mutely passive but immensely effective force against even the slightest policy change. So effective was their resistance that millions of decrees, orders, and requests for information lay unheeded in Russian provincial offices while they continued to perform their mechanical functions in the manner they had learned when they first entered government service.[6]

Between these extremes in Russia's civil service stood those officials who held positions ranging from assistant office section chiefs to department heads. These men implemented policy on a daily basis, knew its flaws from personal observation, and even understood how it might be made more effective or more responsive to particular circumstances. Yet these men feared to make recommendations to their superiors. "They can wipe me from the face of the earth," confessed one such official as he tried to explain why he did not recommend policy changes when he knew they were necessary.[7] Such fears caused men who knew better to tell their superiors only what they thought they wanted to hear. They did not make recommendations that could have made it possible for senior statesmen to propose meaningful changes in policy to the autocrat. And even ministers of state feared to carry criticisms to the Emperor.[8] The result, Valuev confessed in 1855, was that all of Russia's many failings disappeared when one read the official reports. If one believed their contents, he lamented, it seemed that "everything possible has been done everywhere. Success has been achieved everywhere."[9] As Zarudnyi complained at about the same time, the Empire's government was being consumed by a sort of "clerkish rot and ignorance."[10]

A decade before he penned his critique of Russia's administration, Valuev wrote about the officials' obligation to act in a more responsible manner in order to avert a growing paralysis in the Empire's instruments of policy:

> The well-being and domestic success of any state [he wrote to Perovskii in 1845] depends to a significant degree upon the activities of those individuals to whom the more important areas of state administration are entrusted. Their influence on the civil and political life of any country is even more noticeable in an autocratic state, where public opinion stands mute, where citizens are not summoned to participate in discussions of public affairs, and where, finally, great statesmen frequently conceal their personal shortcomings and mistakes behind the impenetrable shield of the autocrat's name.[11]

Although he thought officials should act responsibly, Valuev offered no suggestions about how state policies could be changed, nor did he indicate what new instruments might be created to overcome that near-stalemate between autocracy, aristocracy, and bureaucracy on the issue of changing policy. Like other men who emerged as enlightened bureaucrats in Russia's central administration, Valuev thought it important to assemble information about the government's failings but saw no means for converting those data into new policy.

Failure to convert information into policy was perhaps the most critical issue that progressive officials faced. The most dramatic example was the Committee of December 6th, which failed to institute any changes in policy, even though Nicholas I had given them a broad mandate to survey the entire administration and recommend improvement where they thought necessary.[12] Using especially the testimony of the Decembrists, and admittedly lacking the more accurate data that enlightened bureaucrats assembled two decades later, the committee examined Russia's local and central administration, inquired into the condition of the nobility, and studied the institution of serfdom. Yet they accomplished little. Lack of motivation, far more than lack of information, caused their failure. At Speranskii's urging, they avoided the entire question of changing policy by agreeing that their task was "not the full alteration of the existing order of government, but its refinement by means of a few particular changes and additions."[13] Policy questions thus were transformed into minor administrative issues.

If such august bodies as the Committee of December 6th could not convert new information into new policy, it is not surprising that the bureaucracy as a whole was no more successful. Even on those minor issues about which everyone agreed, it often proved impossible to make policy changes. In a classic case, both St. Petersburg and provincial officials in Zablotskii's agency agreed to improve the quality of sheep that the state peasants raised in southern Russia. Yet some eight years after the work began, the ministry had been unable to put the decision into effect and finally set the entire question aside until some later, unspecified date.[14]

Obviously, some steps had to be taken to create new policy-making instruments in Russia's central administration if the Empire's more crucial and controversial social and economic dilemmas were to be confronted effectively. The need for new policy-making instruments was all the more necessary because the more traditional means for changing policy had proved so ineffective. Both Alexander I's "Unofficial Committee" and Nicholas's Committee of December 6th had been notable failures. Beyond that, Nicholas had convened ten special committees in an attempt to resolve the economic and social crisis posed by serfdom, and all of them had failed.

Miliutin, Zablotskii, and a number of their associates at first perceived only dimly this need for new policy-making instruments. But their efforts to assemble more accurate and comprehensive data about local conditions in Russia created the means for converting information into policy even before they fully realized what they had accomplished. Most important of all, their willingness to seek out expert advice, even when that meant cutting across jealously guarded lines of ministerial authority, established the prototypes for those committees of experts that drafted the Great Reform legislation. Beginning in the mid-1840s, they exchanged information informally.[15] At first such exchanges were confined within a particular department, then broadened to a given ministry, and soon bridged the gap between the ministries that had been created when senior Nicholaean statesmen had refused to sanction formal inter-agency cooperation in a jealous effort to preserve their personal power and authority. The enlightened bureaucrats called this ever-widening process *glasnost'* (literally, publicity), but, as Alexander I and his Young Friends had done with the term "constitution," they endowed it with a meaning quite different from the one it usually bore in the West. At mid-century, the enlightened bureaucrats saw *glasnost'* as a means to involve men who shared their views in a broader discussion of their nation's renovation and transformation. Although limited to specific problems and areas of policy, *glasnost'* became important in bridging the gap between the bureaucracy and educated society which Nicholas I's firm suppression of the Decembrists had opened at the beginning of his reign.

Concern about making qualitative judgments and their increased support of *glasnost'* produced subtle but important changes in the enlightened bureaucrats' attitudes. They no longer emphasized more precise regulations but began to use much more frequently the term "transformation" *(preobrazovanie)* in their discussions of state problems. *Preobrazovanie* had been used by Russian administrators throughout the first half of the nineteenth century, but generally in the narrower sense of administrative or institutional adjustments, even when related to social and economic issues.[16] Zablotskii used it in 1841 to argue that "changes in serfdom ought to change this [present] order of things and should lead to other fundamental transformations in our civic order"[17] but did not describe the transformations to which he alluded, and, from Miliutin's similar usage of the term early in 1844, it seems that both applied it in its traditionally more limited administrative sense. Certainly in his lengthy memorandum "On the Transformation of Municipal Public Administration," Miliutin spoke only of administrative changes in town and city government and did not attach that broader meaning it would have for enlightened bureaucrats a few years later.[18]

V. A. Tsie was probably the first among the enlightened bureaucrats to use *preobrazovanie* in the sense of social or economic transformation, and he did so in the context of his ideas about prison reform. Born in 1820, Tsie graduated from the Lyceum at Tsarskoe Selo the year after Konstantin Veselovskii and entered the civil service as a censor in 1839. In 1847 or 1848 (it is not possible to date the manuscript more precisely), he wrote a brief essay "On Prisons and Their Transformation" in which he urged the rehabilitation of criminals so that valuable human resources would not be lost to the state. "The transformation of prisons is not the consequence of any particular philosophical theory," Tsie wrote. "It is the essential, inevitable requirement of our times . . . [in which] the modernization of our ways, as a result of broader education, urgently requires the abolition of those crude and brutal concepts and customs that have been handed down to us from the middle ages."[19] Tsie argued that the rehabilitation of prisoners was in the best interests of the state and thus specifically tied education and progressive policies to its well-being.

Tsie discussed the transformation of prisons in terms of the state's welfare because the enlightened bureaucrats put the interests of the state before those of any particular group. They used their concern for the welfare of the state to justify much of their statistical work, as Miliutin, Girs, Kavelin, and Redkin characterized their studies of Russia's towns and cities as "a rich collection of practical data and important documents that are essential for the intended transformation [of municipal economy and administration]."[20] Their concern for the state's welfare also led Russia's enlightened bureaucrats, and especially Zablotskii and his associates in the Ministry of State Domains' Academic Committee and Department of Rural Economy, to urge further measures for a gradual transformation of rural Russia during the last decade of the Nicholas era.

For enlightened bureaucrats, the broad issue of rural Russia's transformation during the late 1840s and early 1850s centered on the issue of agricultural improvement; they did not argue for the immediate abolition of serfdom, even though they all considered it an anachronistic and economically unprofitable system. Even to begin the improvement of Russian agriculture was a difficult task because that deep-seated conservatism common to all peasants for whom the failure of new crops or techniques could mean starvation led serfs to resist innovation. In the Russian countryside, such conservatism was institutionalized in the repartitional peasant commune in which a timid or conservative majority could bar a more adventurous minority from experimenting with change. Equally important, the vast majority of Russia's serf-owning nobles were unwilling to diversify crops and did not have the capital to acquire modern agricultural implements. In any case, serfs traditionally supplied the implements with which they tilled the land.

Certainly, any innovation was beyond the means of most Russian serf-owners. According to Keppen's calculations, 84 percent of them owned fewer than 100 male serfs in 1834, and 60 percent owned fewer than twenty. Among these 106,637 serf-owners, the average number of male peasants owned was a mere 18.8, far fewer than the number needed to support a nobleman and his family.[21] For such marginally endowed squires, manorial economy was directed toward survival, not profit and growth. They remained buried in their rural nests, for they could afford to live nowhere else. At best, they hoped to keep themselves afloat with the help of state loans for which their few serfs served as collateral.

If any modernization of age-old agricultural techniques was beyond the means of most serf-owners, that small minority of comfortable-to-wealthy lords, that 16 percent of the serf-owners who owned 81 percent of the serfs, also had little motivation to modernize their estate economy during the Nicholas era.[22] These great lords counted their bondsmen in the hundreds and thousands, and serfdom continued to provide them with a comfortable income. In hard times, they readily could supplement their incomes by state loans, and they preferred the certainty of crops and methods proved over centuries to innovations that were as yet untested.[23] A number of the great lords, whose paths the enlightened bureaucrats crossed in the course of their government assignments, spoke knowledgeably about modern principles of agronomy, the wonders of horse- and steam-driven machinery, and even the inevitability of emancipation; but very few had any intention of putting their preachings into practice.[24] Still, the enlightened bureaucrats' early attempts to set a transformation of rural Russia into motion are instructive, not merely for what they attempted immediately but for what these efforts reveal about their attitudes toward change, the peasantry, the nobility, and, most of all, serfdom, as they probed life in Russia's provinces and laid the foundations for the transformations they knew must come.

Studying Russia's Provinces

During the 1840s, Russia's central administration began to concentrate its resources on studies of provincial life. Such originated with Kiselev's surveys of the state peasantry during the late 1830s and in the Statistical Section that Bludov established in the Ministry of Internal Affairs in 1835, even though inadequate funding at first prevented it from functioning properly.[25] Perovskii hastened to allocate more resources to statistical studies, and in March 1842, he established the Provisional Section for the Reorganization of Municipal Government and Economy for studying economic, social, and administrative conditions in Russia's towns and cities. At about the same time, he assigned the task of compiling broader studies about provincial life to another new agency, the Provisional Statistical Committee.[26] The activities of these two agencies were further coordinated in the 1840s by Miliutin, who directed the Provisional Section and served prominently as a member of the Provisional Statistical Committee. Combined with Zablotskii's Department of Rural Economy in the Ministry of State Domains, they produced impressive studies about life in Russia's provinces during the 1840s and 1850s.

In Russia's central administration, the frequent cooperation of these agencies was particularly unique. At a time when government offices generally were extremely sensitive about their prerogatives and jealously guarded their areas of responsibility, these three bureaus exchanged information and personnel on a continuing basis and without rancor. Men who served in Zablotskii's Department of Rural Economy transferred to Miliutin's Municpal Section in the mid-1840s, and, in some cases, moved back a few years later. Because these agencies were instrumental in providing senior officials in Russia's central administration with reliable information about provincial conditions, we should examine their activities more closely.

When Perovskii assumed office late in 1841, his first concern was with Russia's towns and cities. These had presented serious problems to Imperial statesmen since the time of Peter the Great as senior officials struggled to provide the services urban residents required. These problems were made especially difficult because Russian rulers had begun to create a more modern bureaucratic structure in the central government, while town and city administration continued to function as it had in the seventeenth century.[27] When the *nakazy* drafted for the Legislative Commission of 1767 by its urban constituencies revealed how far city government had diverged from the laws, Catherine II had been obliged to give serious attention to its improvement and issued her Municipal Charter on April 21, 1785.[28] Catherine's charter suffered the fate of earlier eighteenth-century municipal legislation. During the next half-century, the problems that she had attempted to resolve grew worse, and, by the 1840s, Russia's municipal administration had ceased to function effectively.[29] The military governor of Kazan reported that many public offices were staffed by untrained, often illiterate men, leaving a handful of inefficient and corrupt clerks to represent the government in public, while reports from the civil governors of Saratov, Tula, and Poltava confirmed that the situation was equally bad in other areas.[30] Clearly, municipal affairs required serious and immediate attention.

Eighteenth- and early nineteenth-century autocrats faced mainly administrative and economic problems in Russia's cities, but Nicholas I also had to confront social, even political, difficulties. Recent Soviet studies have argued that Russian authorities had become concerned about the growth of an urban proletariat as early as 1826 and feared its political consequences.[31] Although such arguments exaggerate the significance of the government's early efforts to restrict industries located in the larger cities of the Empire, there can be no doubt, as Professor Zelnik has shown in his penetrating study about St. Petersburg's factory workers,[32] that senior officials and the Emperor were apprehensive about an urban proletariat, even though it was not a primary factor in determining their attitudes toward industrial development. During the 1830s, their concern about the social problems heralded by even limited industrial development increased, and, in 1840, Nicholas established a commission chaired by Count P. F. Buxhoeveden to study the conditions under which the "working people and artisans" of St. Petersburg lived and worked. Since there was no government policy about factory workers at that time, Buxhoeveden's Commission was to propose "possible ways to improve their situation."[33] Like most attempts to generate policy within the Nicholaean government, the Buxhoeveden Commission proposed nothing beyond administrative adjustments, and never even finished its work.

Since the beginning of the nineteenth century, five special commissions had been established within the Ministry of Internal Affairs to study urban society and investigate the failings of Russia's municipal government institutions. Like the Buxhoeveden Commission, none had completed their assignment because senior statesmen did not understand the sorts of resources needed for such a task. "This commission is made up of *chinovniki* [who are] occupied with other tasks and who do not receive any additional salary for taking on these extra duties," Perovskii wrote in explaining why the last of these commissions, which he was about to close early in 1842, must be considered a failure like its predecessors. He quickly went on to point out that it lacked the minimum personnel and support services needed to carry out assignments. Unless that was changed, Perovskii insisted, there was no reason to expect that any future effort would be more successful.[34]

Realizing that statistical studies ought to be entrusted to experts able to give them their full attention, Perovskii urged Nicholas to establish the Provisional Section for the Reorganization of Municipal Government and Economy in his ministry. Following the example of Kiselev's recent surveys, he planned to send officials from this new agency to carry out on-the-spot studies of local conditions, and he appointed Miliutin to direct its staff of twenty-six with an annual budget of 13,454 silver rubles.[35] Between 1842 and 1846, Miliutin's new agency concentrated on towns and cities in the provinces of Saratov, Voronezh, Iaroslav, Tula, Riazan, Mogilev, Tambov, and the Baltic regions, in addition to Moscow and St. Petersburg.[36] In all, his agents of special commissions assembled data about municipal budgets, property holdings, and administrative problems[37] in 139 towns and cities.[38]

The very basic economic and administrative data that these surveys emphasized proved hard to come by.[39] Miliutin's agents found it difficult to explain how towns and cities might resolve their fiscal difficulties,[40] because sometimes they could not learn even the most elementary facts about what had caused them. Miliutin bombarded his agents with requests for information about the number of merchants, fairs, shops, and warehouses, the average cost of basic goods and services, and, even, accurate population figures for various towns.[41] Even in Dorpat, home of one of the Empire's great universities, Miliutin had to ask his agent of special commissions for "an enumeration of city dwellers according to their economic status" and for information about the number of bookshops, schools, and charity organizations in the city.[42]

Rudimentary though they were, these early surveys provided training experiences for the new type of officials that Russia's first enlightened bureaucrats were trying to assemble in their agencies. Miliutin insisted that his agents of special commissions and the personnel in the central office of the Provisional Section be far better educated than the average Petersburg official, and it is clear that a substantial portion had elite or university educations. Of those who served prominently in the Provisional Section during the 1840s, Aleksandr Girs, Konstantin Grot, and Konstantin Veselovskii were *litseisty*; Count A. K. Sivers was a *pravoved*; A. F. Shtackelberg and G. I. Frolov were graduates of St. Petersburg University; N. P. Bezobrazov had a degree from the University of Kazan; and K. A. Krzhevitskii held a master's degree from the University of Dorpat. Later in the decade, more illustrious names appeared: Konstantin Kavelin, Ivan Aksakov, Iurii Samarin, Petr Redkin, and Ivan Turgenev all served in Miliutin's Provisional Section before 1850.[43]

But Miliutin demanded far more than advanced education from the men who served under him. They had to abandon the Russian bureaucrat's traditional commitment to formalism[44] and be willing to devote long hours to the drudgery of statistical compilations, as Miliutin insisted on initiative and turned an unsympathetic ear to pleas of overwork. For those who shared his dedication, his demands were welcome;[45] for those who did not, his expectations seemed appalling. "I do not ask you, Your Excellency, I implore you to put yourself in my position," the clearly miserable *tituliarnyi sovetnik* N. V. Kopaneishchikov complained to Miliutin's superior. "I hardly have time to sleep. I must see and verify everything myself, prepare reports, deal with local authorities, and, finally, I now am instructed to attend meetings of the Provincial Council."[46] Such a reaction was the opposite from that of Adolf Shtackelberg who, when asked to determine why trade and industry had declined so precipitously in the Baltic provinces, undertook an additional study on his own initiative about the causes and consequences of famine in the same region.[47]

Once these preliminary studies were completed, and after the St. Petersburg Municipal Reform Act had been drafted, Miliutin broadened his agency's inquiries. During his first years as head of the Provisional Section (renamed the Municipal Section in 1847), he had developed basic data about provincial towns and cities and had assembled a cadre of well-trained, energetic officials in his agency. By the mid-1840s, the Municipal Section had begun to project an image among the intelligentsia and educated elites in Russia that was sufficiently appealing to attract some of the most talented entrants into St. Petersburg's official world. In September 1848, Konstantin Kavelin became an editor in the Municipal Section,[48] and in April of the following year, Miliutin chose the jurist P. G. Redkin to be one of his office section chiefs.[49] Two of the men who had so inspired students at Moscow University earlier in the decade thus placed their talents at Miliutin's disposal before the 1840s ended.

An article in an 1844 issue of *The Journal of the Ministry of Internal Affairs* pointed out that "in both the civic and governmental sense, the city has always been the most noble member of the state's body."[50] Throughout the decade, the efforts of the Municipal Section testified to its officials' belief in that axiom. Excluding Poland and Finland, 693 localities in the Empire bore the designation of *"gorod,"*[51] and, by 1849, Miliutin's agents had studied about 300, despite a number of problems caused by the agents' inexperience and even naïveté at the outset. They had been slow to realize that data housed in provincial archives were so unreliable that accurate information had to be assembled only through first-hand observation,[52] and it was not until after he completed draft proposals for the St. Petersburg reform in 1845 that Miliutin had worked out comprehensive instructions for the studies his agency required. These indicated that he and his associates finally had realized the full extent of their task and had reached conclusions about how it should be undertaken. Miliutin assigned three major duties to his agents of special commissions: "to study existing problems and identify areas in the civic and economic organization of towns and cities in which practice does not conform to the law, to lay the groundwork for compiling complete administrative statistics about these areas of concern, . . . and to seek the means for better organizing civic and economic affairs in these municipalities."[53] In contrast to his earlier instructions, he now urged them to cast the nets of their inquiries widely in order to understand better the nature of municipal society, economy, and administration itself.[54]

Such demanding assignments kept Miliutin's agents of special com-
missions in the provinces for months, even years, in order to complete
them. Adolf Shtackelberg, one of the earliest recruits in the Municipal
Section, spent nearly all of the decade between 1842 and 1851 in the
Baltic provinces,[55] and Girs worked for over two years in Iaroslavl.[56]
Konstantin Grot spent five months in Minsk, six in Tver, and shorter
periods in Kazan, Saratov, Iaroslavl, Poltava, and Mitau.[57] Nikolai
Bezobrazov stayed for nearly three years in Saratov province,[58] K. A.
Krzhevitskii was in the provinces of Kiev, Podolia, and Volynia for over
a year,[59] and Count A. K. Sivers spent some two years in Iaroslavl and
another six months in Tver.[60] Young Count Dmitrii Tolstoi served for
three years in the Baltic provinces and spent another two in Voronezh,
Riazan, Tambov, and Kaluga,[61] while Konstantin Veselovskii worked
for more than a year in Mogilev,[62] as did Ivan Aksakov in Iaroslavl.[63]
These men had to work under arduous conditions, and their lives were
further complicated by the suspicions—sometimes unconcealed hos-
tility—of local officials who saw these deep probings into local economic and administrative practices as direct threats to their long-held
sinecures.[64] Finally, because administrative ties between St. Petersburg
and the provinces were so poorly established, some of these men received their salaries irregularly at best and often lived lives of want
while they waited for their salaries to arrive.[65]

That men of education and culture took up such arduous tasks
bespeaks a devotion to duty that was rare in the Russian bureaucracy.
As Zablotskii remarked some years later, his colleagues saw "in the
fulfillment of their duty . . . a basic law of morality."[66] They also found
an opportunity for worthwhile service to their country at a time when,
as Aksakov lamented to Miliutin, "any sort of civic activity in literature
is impossible."[67] Equally important, as a Municipal Section report stated
in the late 1840s, they had concluded that "these studies will supplement in one of the most critical areas of government, detailed administrative statistics, which represent a rich collection of practical data and
important documents, that are essential for the intended transformation
of . . . all types of state administration."[68]

Municipal Section officials understood that transformations in any
area of Russian life demanded accurate data upon which planners could
base recommendations for change, but they had not yet perceived that
there were no effective instruments for changing policy in Russia's
central bureaucracy. Nonetheless, the more careful allocation of resources and more accurate budgeting procedures that they imposed on
those town and city administrations they studied began to turn large
budget deficits into surpluses. In 1840, public debts in Russia's town and
city governments totalled 260,966 silver rubles and were increasing at

the rate of more than 5 percent a year. Many towns and cities could not provide even basic public services without state subsidies and paid such miserable salaries that they could not hope to engage competent personnel to perform essential services. Regular members of fire-fighting units in some towns, for example, received an annual salary of only 2.86 rubles![69] Miliutin's efforts reversed this trend so significantly that the treasuries of Russia's towns and cities reported a surplus of 370,833 silver rubles in 1847.[70] Even such a limited achievement showed Miliutin and his colleagues that small committees of experts might draft effective reform legislation and pave the way for changing policy in a bureaucracy dedicated to perpetuation of existing policy, not its alteration.

Some two decades later, Zablotskii remarked that Miliutin thought statistics were "the key to administration" and added that "all statistical work done . . . under his supervision always had a practical purpose. These studies broadened as the sphere of his administrative activity expanded."[71] The implications of this work thus extended well beyond the Municipal Section's primary concern for Russia's towns and cities. It gave support to the demands of Zarudnyi and his associates in the Ministry of Justice that *zakonnost'* (lawfulness) be instituted in all areas of Russian life. The acute absence of *zakonnost'* in urban administration, Miliutin argued, was due to local officials' lack of training in the law and the incomprehensibility of the *Digest of the Laws* to all but trained specialists. "The system, and even the editing procedures, used in our *Digest of the Laws* and in all other codices," he wrote, "can be understood only if one possesses a considerable level of judicial education."[72] Miliutin insisted that city officials could not be expected to defend *zakonnost'* until they had convenient access to the laws and assigned N. V. Varadinov, an official who held a doctoral degree in law, to prepare a digest of all resolutions and decrees that applied to municipal administration and government.[73] Varadinov also prepared a lengthy work on the theory and practice of administrative affairs *(deloproizvodstvo)* which, for the first time, provided Russian bureaucrats with a practical guide, a theoretical justification, and an historical explanation for the administrative procedures that ruled their lives and the affairs of the Empire.[74]

The work of Miliutin and his agents extended to other areas, which added other important dimensions to the Municipal Section's activities at mid-century. By the mid-1840s, Kavelin, Miliutin, Redkin, and Girs agreed that serfdom was a malignancy that underlay Russia's economic, social, and political problems and hoped for its eventual abolition.[75] As their interest in serfdom grew, these men and their associates used long months spent in Russia's provincial towns to study conditions in the surrounding countryside as well. Although by no means comprehensive,[76] these studies enabled Miliutin to prepare a lengthy report about grain production in which he determined that Russia was the only nation in Europe to produce enough grain for its people and for export.[77] Going a step beyond the work done by Zablotskii two years earlier,[78] he sought measures to eliminate famine and suggested that improved transportation could provide the key.[79] His proposals contained little beyond those recommendations he had made nearly a decade earlier in his more localized study about the region between St. Petersburg and Moscow,[80] but the volume of statistical data he assembled to describe Russia's grain trade and agricultural production was impressive. As such, his report indicated that the growing emphasis on statistical studies in the Ministry of Internal Affairs had begun to yield broader results. These stemmed partly from the studies produced by his Municipal Section, but also from the statistical work undertaken by other agencies. The Statistical Section, which functioned as an adjunct to the Ministry's Council under the directorship of Konstantin Arsen'ev, was particularly important.

The development of such special statistical bureaux within Russia's central administration was a slow and arduous process. Early attempts to establish statistical agencies ended in failure because most senior officials were unenthusiastic about assembling large holdings of statistical data to help in formulating and implementing state policy. At the beginning of the century, only Speranskii called for a statistical section within the Ministry of Internal Affairs, but his effort came to naught because provincial agencies did not submit the necessary data to the ministry's central office. Transfer of Speranskii's Statistical Section to the short-lived Ministry of Police in 1811 brought no improvement, nor did its return to the Ministry of Internal Affairs in 1819. Plans for its reorganization lay unattended in the Committee of Ministers until late 1827, when it was decided to abolish the Statistical Section altogether.[81] The next year that decision was reversed when Nicholas requested the Ministry of Internal Affairs to provide Konstantin Arsen'ev, a professor in the Imperial School of Engineers, with the information needed to prepare a series of lectures about Russian statistics for Nicholas's eldest son and heir. Imperial interest saved the Ministry's Statistical Section, and its future existence was assured.[82]

One historian recently remarked that Minister of Internal Affairs Count Bludov "tried frantically to please [the Emperor], and was in terror of his master's disapproval."[83] Although Nicholas I's interest in statistics compelled him to reorganize his ministry's statistical office and place it under Arsen'ev's direction, Bludov did not understand how it should function, nor did he realize the resources it required. He therefore assigned Arsen'ev a miserly annual budget of just over 7,000 rubles and a miniscule staff of three statisticians and two copyists.[84] Most of the data for the Statistical Section's work were to be supplied by newly established provincial statistical committees, but few ever submitted reports, and those that did so paid scant attention to accuracy.[85]

Between 1835 and 1842, Arsen'ev employed the major publications of his agency to good purpose nonetheless. In particular, he used its two volumes of *Materials for Statistics of the Russian Empire* to argue the case for additional resources to support more research. Professor Karl Herrmann, Arsen'ev's mentor at St. Petersburg's Pedagogical Institute, already had established the framework for such an appeal a decade earlier when he had written that:

> The value of statistics for a government consists in the fact that they indicate what measures it should take in a given situation and, also, hasten their implementation. . . . Without knowing its population, the quality of its fields, the condition of its factories and manufactures, the bazaars in which its peasants sell their products . . . and, finally, without having a precise understanding of the mores and customs of its peasants, it is impossible to administer a village properly. . . . If such statistical data are needed for the proper administration of a small estate, then just think how essential such data are by comparison for the administration of an entire state.[86]

Arsen'ev elaborated on Herrmann's theme in his plea for an expanded program of statistical research. "Statistics . . . constitute the basis of the state's strength," he wrote in the first volume of *Materials for Statistics of the Russian Empire,* but cautioned that much organization and development needed to be done before such studies could play their intended role. "All we have done thus far," he warned, "is not yet ripened fruit but only good seed. It is not yet a work that is completed, but only a good beginning."[87]

Arsen'ev's plea was repeated in even stronger terms in an unsigned review of the second volume of *Materials.* Appearing in *The Journal of the Ministry of Internal Affairs* in 1842, this essay linked the study of statistics with the precepts of Official Nationality:

> Knowledge of one's homeland [the reviewer wrote] stands much higher than many other types of knowledge and, in view of our present general striving for national character *(narodnost')*, such ought to be required of every statesman, civil servant, soldier, estate owner, industrialist, merchant, and, in general, every educated patriot. We shall go even further and say that without a knowledge of these complex and heterogeneous subjects [i.e., sta-

117

tistics] which, in their totality, comprise the basis of a state's strength, our very love of our homeland cannot be fully unselfish and fruitful.[88]

By the early 1840s, that small circle which included Arsen'ev, Miliutin, his closest associates, and the editorial board of *The Journal of the Ministry of Internal Affairs* hailed statistics as an essential adjunct to the adjustment and implementation of state policy. Their urgings finally reached the highest levels of government when Perovskii became Minister of Internal Affairs late in 1841.

Perovskii knew that statistics were important for adjusting and implementing state policy. Convinced that broad and vital questions of change could be dealt with by administrative measures, he nevertheless realized that it was necessary to understand how that administration functioned before trying to adjust it. It was important to understand what impact administrative adjustments would have on provincial society and economy, and Perovskii therefore approved plans for detailed statistical studies of several provinces that Arsen'ev had selected as typical of various types of economic conditions in Russia. He did not assign these new duties to Arsen'ev's Statistical Section, but to the Provisional Statistical Committee, a new agency that he established in 1843 under the direction of Miliutin's patron and director of the ministry's Economic Department M. I. Leks. Leks was an indifferent administrator, and his strongest asset probably was his aversion to disagreeing with anyone.[89] His appointment allowed control of the committee's work to fall into the hands of Miliutin and Zablotskii, neither of whom had the rank and seniority needed to head it themselves.

The Provisional Statistical Committee reduced Arsen'ev's agency to an impotent appendage of the ministry's Council, and Arsen'ev was not even named a member. He toured Russia's provinces[90] but remained outside the mainstream of statistical work in the Ministry of Internal Affairs for the next decade, as other agencies began broader investigations.[91] It is difficult to discover the reasons for his eclipse. The leading Soviet expert has attributed his removal to a fear of his "progressive views" on the part of a "reactionary government."[92] But Miliutin and Zablotskii, both of whom served on the Provisional Statistical Committee, were no less "progressive" than was Arsen'ev, and, in fact, were more so. More probably, it was not Arsen'ev's "progressive views," but his public statements about how statistical data should be applied to policy formulations, that made Perovskii wary about involving him in broader statistical studies. Even those few statesmen who recognized the importance of statistical data and would have agreed with Professor

Herrmann's opinion that their value consisted "in the fact that they indicate to [the government] . . . what measures to take in a given situation"[93] were reticent about making such information available to men outside their immediate offices. A. I. Artem'ev, an official who served on the Provisional Statistical Committee and its successor, the Statistical Committee, once noted that many of its findings, which had been compiled into five large volumes of "Governmental Statistics about Russia," never were published "because of their extensive nature"[94] and, until the late 1860s, even summary statements of the national budget were considered state secrets by the Emperor and his ministers.[95] Arsen'ev's candidly negative comparisons between Russia and the West in terms of the sophistication of their statistical research could only have made his superiors wary about entrusting him with broader responsibilities.[96] Even more important, he urged greater consultation between government and public opinion and called for the veil of secrecy that shrouded the government's acts to be lifted.

> Until the rural serfowner, the merchant, and the factory owner have come to understand their true interests and have accustomed themselves to publicity (glasnost') which, in the beginning, frightens only those timid, short-sighted, and self-seeking individuals who cannot stop from hiding that which, for the welfare of all, ought to be known to everyone . . . it will be impossible for statistics [in Russia] to reach that level of development already achieved in England, France, Prussia, and a few other states of the German Confederation.[97]

Arsen'ev's conspicuous absence notwithstanding, the Provisional Statistical Committee included some of Russia's leading statisticians. Academicians Keppen and von Baer, as well as Nebolsin, Miliutin, Zablotskii, and Nadezhdin, agreed to launch a broad survey of the Empire that would bring together economic, ethnographic, topographic, public health, and administrative data. Each was an expert in at least one of these fields, and they agreed to combine their collective talent to produce an extensive statistical portrait of life in Russia's provinces. They also decided to begin an intensive study of town and country life in the provinces of Iaroslav and Nizhnii-Novgorod.[98]

By 1846, the Provisional Statistical Committee had not even received the allocations needed to send agents of special commissions to Iaroslav and Nizhnii-Novgorod provinces, while its proposed broader survey of the Empire suffered because key committee members had too many other administrative responsibilities. Each assembled considerable data from government sources, but more pressing duties prevented them from compiling the materials into a final report. Once the Petersburg Municipal Reform Act was implemented, Miliutin took over the arduous task of editing his colleagues' data and, in 1850, completed five volumes of "Governmental Statistics about Russia." Reportedly a vast and comprehensive work that interspersed scholarly essays, extensive tables, and a special atlas with detailed data about the nobility, clergy, state peasants, privately owned serfs, and urban residents of Russia,[99] it never emerged from the inner recesses of St. Petersburg's chanceries. Miliutin published a fifty-page summary in the first volume of the Russian Geographical Society's *Collection of Statistical Information about Russia* in 1851,[100] but the rest of this rich statistical description of Russian life at mid-century perished in a fire that destroyed much of the Economic Section archives on May 28, 1862.[101]

The fire of May 1862 also destroyed the Committee's work on Iaroslav and Nizhnii-Novgorod provinces. During 1852 and 1853, two groups of agents of special commissions were sent to these provinces to assemble what official censuses had failed to obtain: a detailed population analysis according to age, sex, class, occupation, and religion, with special attention to Old Believer sects.[102] These so-called "statistical expeditions" included some of Miliutin's closest colleagues in the Municipal Section and some of the ministry's most able officials, especially Count A. K. Sivers, the novelist Melnikov-Pecherskii, and Aleksandr Artem'ev.[103] Those few documents that survived the fire of 1862 are replete with complaints about the problems of locating information in provincial and district offices, but we know very little else about how provincials reacted to these agents. Gogol's portrait of the young noble wastrel Khlestakov, who was mistaken for an agent of the Third Section and was showered with bribes and gifts by corrupt small town officials, comes most readily to mind, but there is little against which one can test this example, except for one rare account that has survived in Artem'ev's diary. This indicates that the reception accorded to the fictional Khlestakov may have been by no means a mere product of Gogol's fertile imagination. As Artem'ev described his arrival in the town of Myshkino on January 15, 1852:

> I stopped at the hotel. After several minutes, the mayor handed me a document which entitled me to lodgings in the home of one Timofei Vasil'evich Chistov, a merchant of the second guild. Another merchant, Oreshnikov, offered me his horses.... They brought me to a lavish residence, parquet, silk, gold—all were scattered everywhere—but utterly without taste. There the mayor met me again: "Ah, so it turns out that I am to lodge with you!" I said. "Just so, little father, Your Excellency, Aleksandr Ivano-

vich!" exclaimed the mayor, as his grey beard thrust itself forward and his eyes twinkled.[104]

Artem'ev's hosts tried to distract his attention but failed, as he assembled information about local officials and the people they governed. Artem'ev's colleagues must have been equally immune to the charms of their provincial hosts because, by 1853, they had assembled a great deal of material. According to Artem'ev, senior officials' principled objections to the release of Miliutin's broader studies did not extend to statistical information about individual provinces,[105] but funds could not be found to publish the first part of their study until 1861. Entitled *On the Composition and Movement of Population in the Provinces of Nizhnii-Novgorod and Iaroslav,* this work and much of the still-unpublished research were destroyed by the fire of 1862 before any of it was put on sale. A summary, entitled *A List of Populated Locations in Iaroslav Province,* was published somewhat later, in 1865.[106]

By the early 1850s, the efforts of a few enlightened bureaucrats had freed Russia's central administration for the first time from the need to rely on information compiled by suspicious and fearful local officials.[107] Data about provincial economic, administrative, and social conditions thus were assembled in those agencies of the central government that could understand and draw conclusions from them. Perhaps even more important, the work of the Municipal Section and Provisional Statistical Committee took highly educated, well-trained men into the provinces for long periods, which allowed them to gain a first-hand understanding of provincial conditions that was rare in the middle levels of the central administration. This proved particularly valuable when some of these men began to draft legislative proposals for emancipating the serfs and reforming local administration a decade later.

Because the Provisional Statistical Committee cut across ministerial organizational lines, with members from the Ministry of Internal Affairs, the Ministry of State Domains, and the Academy of Sciences, it became especially important in the exchange of information about provincial life within the central bureaucracy. The data assembled in Zablotskii's Statistical Section in the Department of Rural Economy in the Ministry of State Domains broadened that exchange still further. Originally named the Third Department, the Department of Rural Economy was organized on January 1, 1838.[108] Other sections of the ministry were concerned primarily with collecting taxes and levying recruits from state peasant villages, but it worked to improve agriculture in Russia and to broaden the ministry's knowledge about rural life. Its areas of responsibility included cadastral surveys and the direction of agencies charged with disseminating information about agriculture.

Particularly important, the Academic Committee of the Ministry, presided over by the department's chief, operated under its aegis.[109]

As one of the first men to serve in it recalled, the Department of Rural Economy was remarkably unencumbered by clerical assignments. From the very first, its officials were known for their knowledge about rural economy and peasant affairs. These included N. A. Zherebtsov (its vice-director from 1841–1844), A. K. Girs, N. I. Tarasenko-Atreshkov (author of several brochures on economic affairs), A. I. Levshin (an important figure in the preliminary emancipation discussions in the Ministry of Internal Affairs), Keppen, and Zablotskii, as head of the department's Statistical Section.[110] One observer remarked that these men caused the Department of Rural Economy to function "not according to general rules of officialdom, but according to principles of knowledge and enlightenment."[111] Using to good advantage the Emperor's decree of 1839, which permitted only the highest ranking graduates to begin their civil service careers in St. Petersburg, these men launched a concerted effort to entice the elite of Russia's university graduates into their department.[112]

We shall discuss further on the efforts of the Department of Rural Economy and the Academic Committee of the Ministry of State Domains to establish peasant schools and model farms, encourage local agricultural societies, and support agricultural exhibitions. What concerns us here are the statistical studies that these bureaux, and especially Zablotskii's Statistical Section, produced during the 1840s and early 1850s. Based on an on-going series of cadastral surveys begun in the early 1840s, these revealed that although state peasants were taxed on the basis of revisional male souls, as Peter the Great had decreed, they had preserved their tradition of distributing their tax obligations according to the amount of land used by each household.[113] In view of this very common practice, Kiselev and his advisers decided to conduct a thorough examination of state peasants' resources, with an eye to shifting the tax base to the land itself. Special cadastral commissions under the jurisdiction of the Department of Rural Economy were sent into the provinces to classify the fertility of peasant lands, to tabulate the number of labor days required to cultivate a *desiatina* of land in various districts of each province, to chart grain prices, and to estimate levels of peasant literacy.[114]

Begun in May 1842, surveys of state peasants' lands continued into the early 1850s. By 1856, studies of 5,022,725 male souls and 24,710,606 *desiatiny* of land had been completed in twenty-five Great Russian provinces.[115] The result equalized the tax burden on all peasants in all provinces and, according to the official history of the Ministry of State Domains, increased state revenues by six million rubles annually without raising the tax rate.[116] Using the data assembled by these cadastral commissions, the Department of Rural Economy studied the causes of poverty among state peasants and attempted to discover ways to alleviate it. Zablotskii's officials also thought accurate statistical data the key to solving economic and administrative problems. "It is most important of all for administrators to know precisely the subject they are dealing with," Keppen wrote in 1846. "For men responsible for finding ways to improve the economic life of Russia, each piece of information has its value." But Keppen also had begun to urge his younger colleagues to look for trends and set their data into broader contexts. "Information of this type," he explained, "is all the more valuable when it is arranged in a systematic manner, such as in the form of a complete survey of some part of the country."[117] Konstantin Veselovskii, who later replaced Zablotskii as head of the Statistical Section, seconded Keppen's urgings. In addition to statistical data, he insisted, "qualitative evaluations" of economic and social questions were important, for only in that way was it possible to obtain "an accurate appraisal of the status of the subject [under consideration] and . . . reach conclusions about the best means for improving it."[118]

Although the Ministry's cadastral surveys were not completed by the middle of the century, they provided the Department of Rural Economy and its sub-sections—the Academic Committee and the Statistical Section—with enough data for its officials to formulate broader generalizations about provincial conditions and to propose limited measures for bettering the economic position of the state peasants. Perhaps most notable among these commentaries was the "Memorandum on the Shortcomings of Communal Landholding and the Advantages of Private Ownership of Land by the Peasants," which Zablotskii prepared in 1851. When any discussion of change could prove dangerous, Zablotskii began his memorandum with bold proclamation:

> A subject such as the improvement of the economy, by its very nature, and especially in view of that special form in which it exists among us, requires . . . that one take into account those *economic* and *moral* conditions which serve as the basis of the present economic way of life among the peasants.
>
> Among these economic conditions, the *means of owning land* occupies a major place. Without the confidence of the peasant in the continual ownership of those lands which he tills, there can never be any successes in agriculture and all other efforts at improvement will be rendered impotent.[119]

Zablotskii now argued more forcefully than he had a decade before that communal use of land lowered agricultural output and insisted that it was the "stumbling block to any attempt at improvement."[120] His de-

The Winter Palace (Courtesy of the Saltykov-Shchedrin Public Library, Leningrad)

partment's cadastral surveys had convinced him that peasant productivity would increase if the peasant could consider the land his own, but he refrained from the fateful word "emancipation" and even warned that it could prove dangerous to abolish suddenly the age-old custom of communal land usage in peasant villages. The first steps toward improvement should include "gradually introducing new customs and lawfulness *(zakonnost')* in place of absolute confusion and arbitrariness."[121] Therefore, without actually proposing emancipation, Zablotskii urged that state peasants be given private ownership of the fields they tilled and the meadows they used for grazing their cattle and harvesting fodder.[122]

Zablotskii was seeking an eventual transformation of rural Russia so that state peasants would have a more direct stake in the existing order. Perhaps most significant, he, Miliutin, and a number of their associates attempted to involve a broader segment of educated opinion in discussing this gradual transformation, and they did so at a time when the domestic policies of the Nicholas state had reached their most reactionary point. Their most obvious ally was the Russian Geographical Society, but the Department of Rural Economy, and especially its Academic Committee, went even further outside the bureaucracy to assemble information about rural life. In a competition designed to draw educated

Russians into a governmental discussion of important economic and social questions, this body invited private individuals to submit "economic-statistical descriptions" of separate provinces or districts in the Empire. "Only greater *glasnost'* can provide a solid basis for future measures for the improvement of this sector of national industry," the Academic Committee announced.[123]

In post-1848 Russia, this bold appeal met with a predictably timid response. Still, it was noteworthy because it occurred at a time when Nicholas and his advisers were especially wary of involving Russia's educated public in any discussion about the peasantry and change. At the same time, the enlightened bureaucrats made further attempts to understand how provincial conditions might be improved. During the last decade of the Nicholas era, they pursued several undertakings designed to further encourage a gradual transformation of rural Russia.

Toward Gradual Transformation of Rural Russia

Throughout the 1830s and 1840s, grain shipments comprised just over 17 percent of Russia's total exports, and, by 1860, they had risen to almost 36 percent. In 1820, only 19.7 percent of Russia's exports were not agricultural products; by 1860, the portion had fallen to a mere 11.1 percent.[124] Given the importance that agricultural products had for Russia's foreign trade, Imperial statesmen found it a matter of some considerable concern that their nation's peasants were actually among the least productive in Europe. During the 1840s, the grain yields averaged 15.7 bushels per acre in France; in Austria, they were 14.1 bushels; in Prussia, 12.2 bushels; but in Russia, a paltry 9.9 bushels.[125] Not only was the average yield very low, but the ratio of grain harvested to seed planted portrayed a tenuous enterprise at best: 7.1 bushels of grain harvested for each bushel sown was the best yield of any state peasant village in the Empire in 1840. The next best was 4.45:1, and only in seven of forty-seven provinces was the ratio 4:1 or better. The average ratio of grain harvested to seed sown in these provinces was a mere 3.21:1, with one province reporting a disastrous 1.9:1.[126]

Problems associated with the low productivity of Russia's peasantry affected not only the Empire's export trade; they also caused serious domestic economic difficulties. Low productivity combined with wretched transportation caused fluctuations in grain prices that were extreme by any standard. The price of grain in 1838 fluctuated between a high of 25 francs 89 centimes and a low of 14 francs 50 centimes per hectolitre in France. The maximum price never was more than twice the minimum anywhere in the West. However, Russia suffered wild price fluctuations throughout the first half of the nineteenth century.[127] In 1804, the fluctuation was 650 percent. In 1843, there was more than a 500 percent variance between the minimum and maximum, and the fluctuations were even more extreme between one part of the Empire and another. In January 1845, one *kul'* (300 pounds) of rye flour cost 7 rubles 50 kopeks in Pskov, while it cost only one ruble in Tambov and Kharkov. Even in the same province, prices soared and plummeted from one year to the next. A *kul'* of rye flour that sold for three rubles in Kursk in 1829 soared to twenty-three rubles by October 1833 and fell to four rubles in 1836.[128]

Any general increase in productivity was of considerable economic and political importance for Russia; yet it was by no means a simple task to modernize agriculture. Serf resistance to innovation stemmed from that deep-seated conservatism common to all peasants for whom the failure of new crops or techniques meant starvation, but it was intensified by the belief that added or different demands on their time and labor violated long-standing tradition. Serfs therefore resisted those few far-seeing noble masters who attempted to introduce new crops, fertilizers, and machinery on their estates. Such efforts were rare because most rural lords made no attempt to alter the medieval tillage of their estates. Few had the capital to finance new crops or machinery, and most nobles were unwilling to risk capital on such ventures if they had it. They did not understand that there were better ways of increasing their estate profits than to decree increases in *obrok* or bring a few additional *desiatiny* of land under cultivation by adding additional *barshchina* to their serfs' labor obligations.

To overcome this widespread aristocratic indifference to agricultural modernization, a number of enlightened bureaucrats joined a few senior officials in the 1840s in launching a two-pronged program for a gradual transformation of rural Russia. On the one hand, they tried to acquaint more nobles with new advances in agricultural techniques, and they encouraged the development of agricultural societies on the district, provincial, and regional levels to publicize such innovations. At the same time, because they were reluctant to interfere directly in the management of the nobles' affairs, they tried to set a progressive example by the way in which they dealt with the peasants who resided upon Treasury lands. This was a major motivation behind Kiselev's administrative reforms in the late 1830s, and it lay behind the educational programs and model farms with which the government tried to educate its peasants in the 1840s and early 1850s.

The study of agriculture and the training of agronomists was one of those rare areas of education that the autocrat left for a long time in private hands, partly because the formal training of agronomists received little attention anywhere in Russia before the 1840s. Serf-owners usually left agricultural matters to estate managers or to the serfs themselves, and, until the 1820s, there was little effort made to alter traditional forms of serf tillage. The Free Economic Society, founded by Catherine II in 1765, often discussed agricultural questions, and a handful of private agricultural societies had been established at the beginning of the nineteenth century. But the first Russian agricultural school, established by Moscow's Imperial Agricultural Society, was not founded until 1821, and it remained a lonely pioneer for almost two decades until the first state-supported agricultural training center opened on August 15, 1840.[129] Located in Mogilëv province on the Treasury estate of Gorygoretsk, it included a school for teaching peasant farmers about modern agricultural techniques and a higher level institution for educating agronomists to manage large estates.[130] Fluctuations in state policy, coupled with Ministry officials' uncertainty about its true purpose, made the existence of the Gorygoretsk school precarious for almost a decade. Only in 1848 was its place in Russia's educational system made clear when the school was divided into an Agricultural Institute, with university status to train agronomists, and an Agricultural School *(uchilishche)* for state peasants and selected serfs.[131]

Although their educations varied markedly, depending on whether they studied at the Institute or the *uchilishche*, all students received practical training, at the insistence of the Academic Committee. Clearly, such Academic Committee members as Zablotskii, Veselovskii, and Keppen wanted to educate agricultural specialists, not noble dilettantes,[132] and they urged that several more schools be founded in other regions of the Empire because "the establishment of new agronomical schools can be so very important to the state."[133] Because they emphasized the value of practical training, the enlightened bureaucrats on the Academic Committee urged the establishment of eight widely dispersed state-directed model farms.[134] The first was organized in Vologda province, some fifty *versty* from the provincial capital, and was followed by others strategically located in the grain-growing provinces of Saratov, Tambov, Mogilëv, Kazan, Kharkov, and Ekaterinoslav.[135]

Peasants between the ages of seventeen and twenty were trained on these model farms in a four-year course of study that included reading and writing, arithmetic, religion, and elementary agricultural theory, in addition to practical training in all aspects of agriculture and animal husbandry. Especially during the winter months, they were trained in a variety of those trades and crafts needed by prosperous peasant farmers, and particular attention was given to blacksmithing and repairing farm implements.[136] Most important, they learned about raising tobacco and fodder crops in addition to the usual grains so that they could practice effective crop rotation when they returned home.[137]

The Academic Committee thus tried to educate at least a small number of peasants in more advanced agricultural techniques. Like most efforts conceived within such bureaucracies, their program suffered from inadequate funding, and they had to develop their model farm program much more slowly than they wished. They had planned to enroll some 75–150 state peasants and 25–50 serfs on each farm in order to train between 800 and 1,600 in any four-year period, but, by mid-century, their limited budget had made it possible to provide housing for only 706.[138] Further, some of the classroom work must have been far too sophisticated for student farmers who had learned to read and write only after they arrived at school. Some of the titles in the farms' student libraries presupposed such advanced education that peasant student farmers could not have even hoped to read them. Apparently, a number of those enlightened bureaucrats who administered Russia's model farm program were unable to comprehend the level at which peasant students must be taught.[139]

Whatever their limitations, the agricultural schools and model farms established by the Ministry of State Domains during the 1840s laid the base for that gradual transformation of rural Russia that enlightened bureaucrats envisioned. These institutions not only taught peasant farmers agricultural techniques and useful trades, but they also trained them in the manufacture of modern farm implements. At the Vologda model farm, for example, more than a dozen different types of farm implements, including steel harrows and self-scouring plows modeled on the design perfected by the Illinois blacksmith John Deere only a few years before, were produced by peasant students at mid-century, and a number of these were taken back to their villages by proud graduates.[140] Small numbers of modern implements thus made their way into the Russian countryside on the eve of the Crimean War; along with them came peasants trained in their manufacture, use, and repair.

That Russia's rural masses were interested in agricultural innovation became even more evident to the enlightened bureaucrats in the Department of Rural Economy as a result of their efforts to organize provincial agricultural exhibitions. Zablotskii and his colleagues saw these as important vehicles for exchanging information, recognizing the accomplishments of able peasants, and improving agricultural productivity. "Public exhibitions of products of the agricultural industry stimulate competition among producers and, at the same time, serve as a means to evaluate the level of development of this or that sector of agricultural labor, as an indication of measures needed for further achievements, and as a means for bringing farmers closer together," the authors of the Department's five-year report wrote in 1849.[141] Their success may well indicate that some of Russia's peasants were considerably less backward than the extremely low overall agricultural productivity figures indicate. This does not mean that the image of primitiveness attached to Russian agriculture in the middle of the nineteenth century lacks validity or that the rural transformation that enlightened bureaucrats envisioned did not lie some considerable distance in the future. But it does indicate that there was enough interest in raising productivity among Russia's rural population to establish the basis for such a transformation. That most exhibitors were state peasants, in whose hamlets the enlightened bureaucrats in the Department of Rural Economy were breaking down the peasant practice of communal land usage,[142] may indicate that the primitive quality of Russian agriculture was more the result of conservatism articulated by the repartitional commune than of individual peasant resistance to innovation and progress.

Russia's first agricultural exhibition was held in Odessa in 1843. When the number of exhibitors increased by nearly 50 percent the following year, officials in the Department of Rural Economy decided that an Empire-wide program of such exhibitions might be successful. They broadened their efforts that same year in Iaroslavl and more than 300 entrants, most of them state peasants and serfs, came to display their exhibits. Again, the number of entrants more than doubled the following year, and the number of exhibits almost reached 7,500.[143]

The successes of these first agricultural exhibitions encouraged the enlightened bureaucrats in the Department of Rural Economy to plan others. During the last decade of the Nicholas era, such exhibitions were held in the provinces of Iaroslav, Tambov, Ekaterinoslav, Kazan, Poltava, Vladimir, Vologda, and Taurida, and each brought entrants from several surrounding provinces. Between 1844 and 1849 alone, they attracted nearly 6,000 exhibitors and had almost three times that number of exhibits.[144] As had been the case in Odessa and Iaroslavl, most entrants were state peasants. As we suggested earlier, this may have indicated a more serious interest in the quality of agricultural production among Russia's masses than historians have realized.

Such enlightened bureaucrats as Zablotskii and his associates in the Department of Rural Economy tried to lay the groundwork for a gradual transformation of rural Russia by training state peasants and serfs and hoped to stimulate interest in modernization through provincial agricultural exhibitions. To support their program further, they encouraged nobles to establish agricultural societies and used them to stimulate discussion about new crops, chemical fertilizers, and agricultural machinery among Russia's provincial lords. They hoped that their effort would help to mechanize Russian agriculture and, in turn, increase crop yields to meet the growing demand for Russian grain in Europe.

Russia's first agricultural society had been founded in 1765, just over a decade after its counterpart had been established in England (1753) and just four years after a similar one had been founded in Paris.[145] Named the Free Economic Society, it included great lords and scientific experts who joined to promote agricultural advancement in Russia.[146] One of their major objectives was to increase the revenues from their estates, but they also hoped to induce smaller proprietors to follow their example.[147] For three decades, they pursued these tasks alone. Then, in 1805, the Baltic lords of Lifland formed an agricultural society; their example was followed in 1818 when the nobility of Moscow founded the Imperial Agricultural Society.[148]

Professor Blackwell has written that the Imperial Agricultural Society at Moscow "particularly reflected the concerns and curiosities of landlords who were turning their production toward commercial markets and who wished to develop and modernize agricultural industries."[149] Their interest was shared by the Free Economic and Lifland Agricultural Societies, but their activities were restricted to the great lords of the Empire, often with close connections at Court. Especially in the case of the Free Economic Society and the Imperial Agricultural Society at Moscow, their endeavors to some extent reflected state policy because they received substantial subsidies from the Ministries of State Domains and Finance.[150] Their leading members often were senior statesmen (Admiral Count N. S. Mordvinov presided over the Free Economic Society for many years, for example), and, although they wrote about their work in journals and scientific texts, even the more prosperous and better educated segments of the Great Russian provincial nobility usually were not closely associated with them.

In an attempt to broaden participation in the improvement of Russian agriculture, Kiselev launched a program to increase the number of agricultural societies even before the Ministry of State Domains was founded. In the late 1830s and early 1840s, the Imperial Economic Society at Kazan (1839), the Iaroslav Agricultural Society (1842), the Estland Agricultural Society (1839), the Kurland Agricultural Society (1839), and the Gol'dingen (Kuldiga) Agricultural Society (1839) were founded, in response to his urging. The latter three centered in the Baltic provinces—an obvious indication of the Baltic German lords' continued interest in agronomy—but the societies at Kazan and Iaroslav, especially when viewed in conjunction with the Imperial Agricultural Society of Southern Russia (founded in 1828), showed that interest in new crops and agricultural techniques had begun to spread among the provincial lords of the South and West.[151]

Enlightened bureaucrats in the Department of Rural Economy encouraged this new interest in agricultural modernization outside the capitals and the Baltic provinces during the late 1840s and early 1850s. Branches of the Imperial Agricultural Society of Southern Russia were established in Ekaterinoslav and Kishinev in 1845, followed by the formation of the Lebedian Agricultural Society (in Tambov province) in 1847 and the Agricultural Society of Southwestern Russia (in Penza) in 1848.[152] But there was strong resistance from many Russian serf-owners, and, although by mid-century there were twenty-one private organizations concerned with agricultural modernization, all but eight were in Moscow, St. Petersburg, or the Baltic provinces.[153]

It is difficult to explain why enlightened bureaucrats in the Department of Rural Economy found it so difficult to win the support of Russia's provincial nobles in their efforts to establish a network of agricultural societies, and they were extremely vague about it in their published remarks. "Unfortunately, it is necessary to note," they wrote in their five-year report in 1849, "that in spite of all the Department's willingness to increase the number of these organizations, obstacles to the formation of local agricultural societies have been encountered in the majority of provinces, the elimination of which does not depend upon the Department."[154] The conservatism of the provincial nobility was undoubtedly a factor in this reluctance, especially when coupled with their very limited capital resources. Still, these factors alone do not adequately explain the reluctance of the provincial lords to form local agricultural societies, and we must look elsewhere for an answer.

There is little archival evidence to suggest to us the process by which enlightened bureaucrats in the Department of Rural Economy initiated debate about the establishment of provincial agricultural societies, and there is even less evidence about local nobles' response. Nonetheless, one can make some inference about the process and the reasons for the reticence of the nobles from events that occurred in Tula in 1846. There, a segment of the nobility fell directly into the group that Professor Blackwell described as "landlords who were turning their production toward commercial markets and who wished to develop and modernize agricultural industries,"[155] and they were quite aware of the economic constraints imposed on their efforts by serfdom.[156] Yet, when urged to organize a provincial agricultural society in 1846, they refused. We have little specific information to explain why they did so, but the proposal itself may provide some accurate clues. When the Tula Provincial Assembly of the Nobility met in 1846, State Councillor Pokhvisnev, Marshal of the Nobility in Venevsk district, suggested that they organize a provincial agricultural society. Pokhvisnev cast his proposal very much in terms of the views held by enlightened bureaucrats in the Department of Rural Economy. Although he spoke about the benefit serf-owners could derive from the information such a society could disseminate, he emphasized how the nobility could serve the throne by forming such a society. "Who among us is not convinced that we are obliged to serve the throne and our homeland to the utmost?" he asked. "Who among the Russian nobility is not prepared to give up his property, even his life, for Tsar and Country?"[157]

A reasonably accurate reply to Pokhvisnev's rhetorical questions might have been "almost no one." In theory, Russia's serf-owners remained the first servants of the throne, but at mid-century reality bore little resemblance to theory. Provincial lords still exalted the virtue of having served as a measure of social respectability rather than as a duty owed to Tsar and Country. Far more important were their estates and their unlimited power over their serfs. "The Emperor can issue his commands to me, and I must obey him, but he issues no commands to you," one observer wrote in recounting a nobleman's speech to his assembled serfs. "I am the Emperor on my estate," he continued. "I am your God in this world and I have to answer for you to the God above."[158] Given this attitude among provincial nobles, one can surmise that the Tula nobility were hardly sympathetic to an appeal that they form an agricultural society to serve Tsar and Country. They probably were even less sympathetic after they learned that one major purpose of the society would be to provide data about their province's serf economy so that government officials could prepare proposals for bettering the conditions under which Tula bondsmen lived.[159] The assembled Tula nobility voted down Pokhvisnev's proposal by a margin of nearly three to one.[160]

Although the evidence is far from conclusive, it suggests that enlightened bureaucrats in the Department of Rural Economy attempted to impose a more responsible view of state service on provincial nobles by urging them to participate in local agricultural societies. That they perceived a purpose in the creation of such societies beyond the betterment of Russia's manorial economy was especially clear in a memorandum that Zablotskii sent to Grand Duke Konstantin Nikolaevich just a few months after the Crimean War ended. After pointing out that they had publicized such issues as new crops, machines, and farming methods but had "accomplished very little in the area of bettering the condition of the serfs,"[161] Zablotskii urged that agricultural societies be brought more closely under the control of his Department of Rural Economy. In that way such societies could play an important part in preparations for an emancipation by "accustoming our society to the idea that the abolition of serfdom is inevitable [and] by ridding this idea of the phantoms and false notions formed by confused imaginations . . . which, until the present time, have clouded the clear understanding of this matter."[162] Zablotskii hoped to initiate a controlled debate on emancipation within Russian society and envisioned agricultural societies, especially those in Moscow and St. Petersburg, as useful instruments through which the government could encourage discussion yet keep it within limits acceptable to the Emperor and his closest advisers. Zablotskii thus saw them as an important element in broadening the process of *glasnost'*.[163]

That these views were not born merely of Zablotskii's concern about Russia's Crimean debacle can be seen from the efforts of the Ministry of State Domains' Academic Committee and Department of Rural Economy to utilize agricultural societies during the first half of the decade. In 1852 and 1853, the Academic Committee invited noble agricultural societies to submit proposals for improving agriculture in Russia, and eleven societies responded at some length. While an overriding concern about the narrowly focused interests of Russia's serf-owners dominated their replies, they exhibited a broad grasp of the agricultural dilemmas their nation faced.[164] Clearly, they viewed the invitation as a far broader mandate for discussion than did the civil servants who initiated the inquiry. Their proposals covered an impressive range of topics and problems, from the need for an "immediate definition of the relations between peasants and their lords," to the shortage of veterinarians in the countryside and the need for cattle insurance,[165] even though Zablotskii and his colleagues thought these societies should confine themselves to providing information needed by the central bureaucracy. As he remarked to Konstantin Nikolaevich, "the cooperation of private individuals, freely given, can be useful and valuable for the government, but, for such private individuals, the support of the government is essential."[166] In his view, that fundamental fact defined the relationship between the two.

Most government officials feared to involve public opinion in discussions of policy, and even such enlightened bureaucrats as Zablotskii and Veselovskii found it difficult to extend their concept of *glasnost'* that far. This was partly because their bureaucratic experience had conditioned them to expect obedience from society, not encourage dialogue with it. The difficult political climate in which they had to work during the first half of the 1850s also was a factor because no one knew just how much discussion of state affairs could be considered legitimate. Finally, enlightened bureaucrats' apprehensions stemmed from their reluctance to discuss solutions when they did not yet fully understand the problem. Fearful that they had gone too far, Zablotskii, Veselovskii, and their colleagues began to parry Russia's agricultural societies with those standard bureaucratic responses they had learned so well. They referred important matters to other agencies and pleaded that they did not have the authority to discuss critical issues. An opportunity to extend *glasnost'* beyond the confines of the bureaucracy thus was lost as a consequence of the enlightened bureaucrats' own inability to pursue a dialogue among groups with whom they were not closely acquainted and whose public statements they could not readily control.

As with Miliutin's timid attempt to extend *glasnost'* to the Petersburg merchantry in 1844, the efforts of Zablotskii and his associates to extend it to Russia's agricultural societies proved unsuccessful. Russian lords proved unwilling to accept the limited role that officials in the Department of Rural Economy offered them, and the enlightened bureaucrats grew uneasy as a result. But it was they, not the nobles willing to discuss policy in concrete terms, who were most responsible for the failure of the attempt. Unfamiliar with the limits to which *glasnost'* could be extended, and unwilling to press their discussions to those limits, the enlightened bureaucrats turned away from the very men whom reasonable debate might have turned into valuable allies.

Enlightened bureaucrats never felt at ease with public opinion, and that produced a growing disenchantment with their programs among the nobility. Many Russian lords would have agreed with General Tsimmerman's statement that enlightened bureaucrats "were in no way advocates of true freedom, which has nothing in common with this stifling sphere of officialistic democracy," and that "once they had obtained power these liberals became unceremonious despots and exercised absolute arbitrariness in their actions."[167] Enlightened bureaucrats' apprehensions stemmed from their conviction that the nobility was selfish and irresponsible. "The nobility is self-interested, unprepared, [and] underdeveloped," Miliutin soon wrote to Kiselev.[168] Based on his own experience, he and his associates had little reason to think otherwise. Therefore, they modified the process of bureaucratic co-optation to extend *glasnost'* beyond the bureaucracy.

Noblemen who entered the bureaucracy and exhibited those abilities that enlightened bureaucrats respected, or those whom they came to know in their Petersburg circles, became the ones with whom they pursued discussions about reform and change. The serf-owner and Slavophile Iurii Samarin in an important sense owed his place on the Editing Commissions to his years of service with enlightened bureaucrats in the Ministry of Internal Affairs, while they withheld such trust from Ivan Aksakov, who had not proved reliable and loyal during his service in Miliutin's Municipal Section. Kavelin won their trust because of his accomplishments in the Municipal Section during the late 1840s and early 1850s, and Prince Cherkasskii gained entry to their inner circle because of his close association with the Grand Duchess Elena Pavlovna, who became a generous patron of the enlightened bureaucrats during the same period.

The efforts of the enlightened bureaucrats to extend *glasnost'* thus took place mainly within the bureaucracy and a few private circles during the last decade of the Nicholas era when they launched the co-optation process that brought a few of the intelligentsia into their ranks. The cadre of reformers whom Miliutin, Zarudnyi, and Zablotskii assembled in their agencies during the mid-1840s had become almost fully developed by 1855, and its ranks expanded very little during the next decade. It was the enlightened bureaucracy, as formed by the end of the Crimean War, that played a major part in planning Russia's Great Reforms, and it was to the men who proved themselves during the last decade of the Nicholas era that they turned to help them draft reform legislation. Especially in the preparations for reform in the Polish Kingdom in 1863–1866, Miliutin first turned not to men with government service experience in Poland but to those who had been tested in the bureaucratic arena during the last decade of the Nicholas era.

During this period of the Nicholas era, Russia's emerging enlightened bureaucrats thus became more deeply involved with problems of transformation and change than one might expect, in view of the reactionary character that has been assigned to that period of the Empire's history. It is true, of course, that they shared apprehensions held almost universally among men who favored reform, and, like their friends among St. Petersburg's intelligentsia, they were reluctant to discuss reform questions openly. Like most educated Russians, they stood ready to condemn the excesses of revolution in western Europe by mid-1848, but they had to be more cautious in expressing their political opinions because the Emperor demanded that government officials set the standard of loyalty by which others were measured. Writers who ran afoul of the censors were dealt with more severely if they were in the civil service, as Dal' and Saltykov-Shchedrin could readily testify. Those who feared to tread that narrow and blurred line between the acceptable and the forbidden retreated for fear of damaging their ability to influence state affairs at a later and more propitious time.[169]

These added risks made it all the more remarkable that some of the enlightened bureaucrats pursued their program for a gradual transformation of rural Russia throughout the dark days after 1848. They could do so because their perceptions about Russian politics were more acute than those who shunned careers in the bureaucracy. Schooled in the hard realities of Petersburg intrigue for more than a decade, the enlightened bureaucrats had acquired highly sensitive political instincts. They had risen in the civil service precisely because their education, talent, and willingness to approach state affairs from a nontraditional outlook had attracted such energetic and less rigid statesmen as Kiselev and Perovskii who, even after 1848, shielded them from the worst dangers of Russia's capricious political climate. At mid-century, they began to attract the attention of even more illustrious protectors. Golovin's privileged position as one of Konstantin Nikolaevich's confidants brought the Grand Duke's protection to his friends, especially after they seized control of the Russian Geographical Society. As President of the Geographical Society, Konstantin Nikolaevich scarcely could deny them his protection, at least by association, so long as they did not violate censorship regulations openly. In that matter, the enlightened bureaucrats were supremely cautious. Between 1848 and 1856, their published writings were exclusively technical or statistical and contained nothing that could be considered objectionable by even the most paranoid of censors.

Grand Duke Konstantin Nikolaevich strengthened the enlightened bureaucrats' defenses, and, as the first half of the 1850s drew to a close, he recruited a number of them into his Naval Ministry. At the same time, Miliutin and Prince Dmitrii Obolenskii found another protector in the person of Grand Duchess Elena Pavlovna, wife of the Emperor's younger brother Grand Duke Mikhail Pavlovich, whose circle, like that of Konstantin Nikolaevich, we shall examine at some length in the next chapter. With support from such highly placed patrons, the political position of the enlightened bureaucrats at the time of the Crimean War was far more secure than that of any other progressive group in Russia.

Enlightened bureaucrats enjoyed patronage in high places not only because of their sharply honed instincts for political survival but because their perspective on state affairs differed from that of other men dedicated to reform and change. Although their outlooks had been influenced by western European idealism, they had become pragmatic and realistic men who understood the futility of proposing theoretical solutions to pressing economic and political problems. They never shared the fascinations with ideal societies—utopian socialist or otherwise—that had so entranced many among Russia's intelligentsia. Necessity had obliged them to jettison such ideological trappings while they struggled to establish themselves in government service. Therefore, they read the works of Proudhon, Fourier, and Louis Blanc,[170] Prince Obolenskii recalled many years later, but their interest was academic. They never seriously thought that such societies could take root in Russia. From their positions within the bureaucracy, they thought that meaningful work in the cause of transformation was possible even after